Learning C for Arduino

A comprehensive guide that will help you ace C's fundamentals using the powerful Arduino board

Syed Omar Faruk Towaha

BIRMINGHAM - MUMBAI

Learning C for Arduino

First published: March 2017

Production reference: 1220317

Published by Packt Publishing Ltd.
Livery Place
35 Livery Street
Birmingham
B3 2PB, UK.

ISBN 978-1-78712-009-9

www.packtpub.com

Credits

Author

Syed Omar Faruk Towaha

Reviewer

Francesco Balducci

Commissioning Editor

Veena Pagare

Acquisition Editor

Mansi Sanghavi

Content Development Editor

Trusha Shriyan

Technical Editor

Naveenkumar Jain

Copy Editor

Safis Editing

Project Coordinator

Kinjal Bari

Proofreader

Safis Editing

Indexer

Mariammal Chettiyar

Graphics

Kirk D'Penha

Production Coordinator

Aparna Bhagat

About the Author

Syed Omar Faruk Towaha has degrees in physics and computer engineering. He is a technologist, tech speaker, and physics enthusiast from Shahjalal University of Science and Technology (SUST), Bangladesh. He has passion for programming, tech writing, and physics experiments. His recent books include Easy Circuits for Kids, Fundamentals of Ruby, How You Should Design Algorithms, and JavaScript Projects for Kids. He is an Oracle-certified professional developer who is currently involved with a number of projects that serve both physics and computer architecture. He is currently working as the CTO of an IT company.

About the Reviewer

Francesco Balducci is a software engineer, working on Digital Signal Processing, micro-controllers, systems-on-chip, and ASIC products, and is currently employed at ST Microelectronics. He received his degree in Electronic Engineering at Politecnico di Torino in 2005. His thesis was about software security and methods to measure the strength of copy protection systems.

www.PacktPub.com

For support files and downloads related to your book, please visit www.PacktPub.com.

Did you know that Packt offers eBook versions of every book published, with PDF and ePub files available? You can upgrade to the eBook version at www.PacktPub.com and as a print book customer, you are entitled to a discount on the eBook copy. Get in touch with us at service@packtpub.com for more details.

At www.PacktPub.com, you can also read a collection of free technical articles, sign up for a range of free newsletters and receive exclusive discounts and offers on Packt books and eBooks.

https://www.packtpub.com/mapt

Get the most in-demand software skills with Mapt. Mapt gives you full access to all Packt books and video courses, as well as industry-leading tools to help you plan your personal development and advance your career.

Why subscribe?

- Fully searchable across every book published by Packt
- Copy and paste, print, and bookmark content
- On demand and accessible via a web browser

Customer Feedback

Thanks for purchasing this Packt book. At Packt, quality is at the heart of our editorial process. To help us improve, please leave us an honest review on this book's Amazon page at https://www.amazon.com/dp/1787120090.

If you'd like to join our team of regular reviewers, you can e-mail us at customerreviews@packtpub.com. We award our regular reviewers with free eBooks and videos in exchange for their valuable feedback. Help us be relentless in improving our products!

Table of Contents

Preface

Have you ever thought about making a robot? Or an electronic device that can be programmed for serving mechanical or logical purposes? If yes, then this book is the perfect guide for you. Throughout this book, you will be guided to learn C programming, which is required to program the microcontroller used in a logical device. You will also learn how you can develop your ideas about making an intelligent device. You will be able to program Arduino for your projects or play with Arduino for fun.

What this book covers

Chapter 1, *Getting Started*, in this chapter, you will learn about Arduino, types of Arduino, Install the Arduino IDE and know the Arduino IDE. This chapter will also have details about the functions of the Arduino IDE software.

Chapter 2, *Our First Program!* in this chapter, you will learn how you can connect your Arduino to the computer and write the first program for the Arduino. You will also learn how you can format your code. A simple Arduino project will also be discussed in this chapter.

Chapter 3, *Exploring C with Arduino IDE*, in this chapter, you will learn about C programming for Arduino. You will learn how you can declare variables, take inputs from the Serial Monitor, few mathematical operations, String, Arrays and many other things related to C programming.

Chapter 4, *Blinking with Operations and Loops*, in this chapter, you will learn logical operations and loops. You will also learn where you can use these techniques in your programs.

Chapter 5, *Functions and Files with Arduino*, in this chapter, you will learn about functions, functions types, and file handlings. You will also learn how you can connect an SD card to your Arduino and program for it to read and write.

Chapter 6, *Arduino and C++*, in this chapter you will learn basic things about object oriented programming, the benefits of OOP, and how you can use OOP in Arduino programming. At the end of this chapter you will be able to connect GSM module to your Arduino and make call or send and receive SMS with the module.

`Chapter 7`, *Using Pointers and Structure*, in this chapter you will go deeper into the C programming. You will learn the usages of pointer and structure. You will also learn how you can use them in your code.

`Chapter 8`, *Working with Arduino Libraries*, in this chapter, you will learn about Arduino libraries. You will learn how you can install a library and use it in your code. You will learn about few famous Arduino libraries.

`Chapter 9`, *Let's Build Something Awesome*, in this chapter, you will build a number of projects including LED cube, a smart weather system, and a home security system. You will also learn how you can make your own projects.

`Chapter 10`, *Few Error Handlings*, in this chapter, you will learn how you can solve few common Arduino errors. You will also learn techniques for fixing errors that can occur in building any project or code.

What you need for this book

Software: Arduino IDE and Fritzing.

Who this book is for

This book is for hobbyists who have no knowledge about programming and microcontrollers, but are keen to learn C programming using a very affordable hardware device.

Conventions

In this book, you will find a number of text styles that distinguish between different kinds of information. Here are some examples of these styles and an explanation of their meaning.

Code words in text, database table names, folder names, filenames, file extensions, path names, dummy URLs, user input, and Twitter handles are shown as follows: "On the last code we have written `Serial.print("Hello Arduino!\n")`."

A block of code is set as follows:

```
void setup() {
  Serial.begin(9600);
}
void loop() {
  Serial.print("Hello Arduino!\n");
}
```

New terms and **important words** are shown in bold. Words that you see on the screen, for example, in menus or dialog boxes, appear in the text like this: "If you go to **Tools | Port** you will see a bunch of port list."

Warnings or important notes appear in a box like this.

Tips and tricks appear like this.

Reader feedback

Feedback from our readers is always welcome. Let us know what you think about this book-what you liked or disliked. Reader feedback is important for us as it helps us develop titles that you will really get the most out of. To send us general feedback, simply e-mail feedback@packtpub.com, and mention the book's title in the subject of your message. If there is a topic that you have expertise in and you are interested in either writing or contributing to a book, see our author guide at www.packtpub.com/authors.

Customer support

Now that you are the proud owner of a Packt book, we have a number of things to help you to get the most from your purchase.

Errata

Although we have taken every care to ensure the accuracy of our content, mistakes do happen. If you find a mistake in one of our books-maybe a mistake in the text or the code-we would be grateful if you could report this to us. By doing so, you can save other readers from frustration and help us improve subsequent versions of this book. If you find any errata, please report them by visiting http://www.packtpub.com/submit-errata, selecting your book, clicking on the **Errata Submission Form** link, and entering the details of your errata. Once your errata are verified, your submission will be accepted and the errata will be uploaded to our website or added to any list of existing errata under the Errata section of that title.

To view the previously submitted errata, go to https://www.packtpub.com/books/content/support and enter the name of the book in the search field. The required information will appear under the **Errata** section.

Piracy

Piracy of copyrighted material on the Internet is an ongoing problem across all media. At Packt, we take the protection of our copyright and licenses very seriously. If you come across any illegal copies of our works in any form on the Internet, please provide us with the location address or website name immediately so that we can pursue a remedy.

Please contact us at copyright@packtpub.com with a link to the suspected pirated material.

We appreciate your help in protecting our authors and our ability to bring you valuable content.

Questions

If you have a problem with any aspect of this book, you can contact us at questions@packtpub.com, and we will do our best to address the problem.

1
Getting Started

Since you have picked this book, this means you want to learn both about programming and electronics, especially microcontrollers. The book is designed to enable you to learn C programming easily and implement the language with an Arduino. I would suggest you do every code of the book by yourself and run them on the Arduino IDE. Microcontroller programming was hard before, but since the innovation of Arduino and the use of C programming on the Arduino board, microcontroller programming has become easy and fun.

Before going any further, let's understand the programming language C better. You may wonder why C programming is called **C**.

Well, before the creation of C, there was its predecessor programming language, called **B**. So, you should be able to guess from this where the name came from. The B language was developed by Ken Thompson at Bell Labs. At the same lab, the C language was developed in 1972 by Dennis Ritchie. The main purpose of creating this language was to design a UNIX operating system. Ken Thomson and Dennis Ritchie were the main developers of the UNIX operating system, so Dennis developed C to design UNIX.

C is not just a powerful language but a flexible one too. It is a portable language, because we can write a C program on one computer and compile to another with almost no modification.

To compile the source code of C, we need to have an IDE installed to our computers. Throughout this book we will learn C programming using the Arduino IDE. We will also be introduced to the Arduino IDE, its installation process, and how we can run our very first C program using an Arduino and the Arduino IDE.

IDE stands for Integrated Development Environment. IDEs are used for software development. An IDE usually consists of an editor (where we can type code and comments), and a few tools along with a debugger (which is used to test the code to see if it has any errors). Most IDEs have a built in compiler (which converts source code/programming language into machine language).

Let's get introduced to an Arduino now.

Arduino

Arduino is a microcontroller board. People also call it a prototype board. In a nutshell, an Arduino board is a small computer with a processor, RAM, ROM etc. Arduino is open source hardware – you might have heard of *open source software*. Open source software is computer software distributed with a license that gives the users the right to see its source code. A Free Open Source Software license provides the rights to study, change and distribute the software to anyone for any kind of purpose. Open source software is usually developed by a group of open source enthusiasts who develop and gradually fix bugs of the software.

Since Arduino is open source hardware, we can build our own Arduino and also develop it for the purpose of our goals. We can change it to whatever we want.

Types of Arduino

Since Arduino is open source hardware, people around the world modify the board according to their needs. There are a few companies that produce different versions and types of Arduino. Let's get introduced to a few famous types of Arduinos.

Arduino Uno

Arduino Uno is the most-used Arduino board. It is based on the ATmega328 microcontroller. It has 14 digital pins and six analog inputs. We will know more about analog and digital pins in the next chapters.

The ATmega328 has 32Kbytes flash memory, 32 pins, 20MHz maximum operating frequency and 8-bit AVR CPU. The following image is an Arduino Uno board and an ATmega328 microcontroller with its pin out:

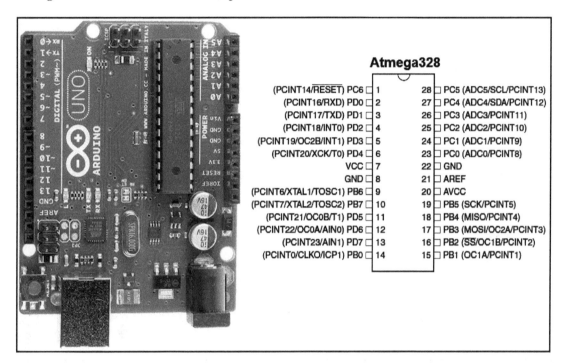

Arduino Mega

Arduino Mega is a microcontroller board that is famous for providing more pins. It uses ATmega2560, and has 54 digital pins and 16 analog inputs.

The ATmega2560 has 256Kbytes of flash memory, 100 pins, 16MHz operating frequency and 8-bit AVR CPU. The following image is an Arduino Mega and an ATmega2560 microcontroller with its pin out:

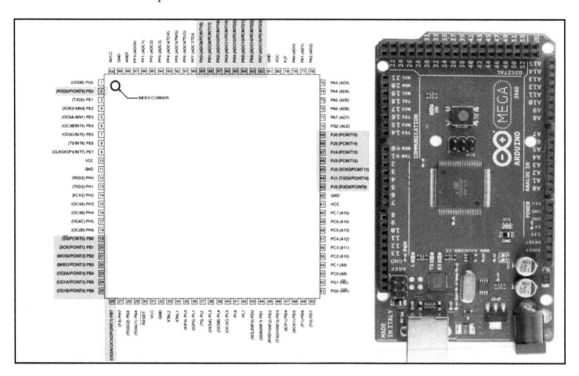

Arduino Nano

Arduino Nano is usually chosen for prototypes with a small form factor. It is based on the ATmega328 microcontroller, which is same as the Arduino Uno. It has 14 digital pins and eight analog inputs. The following image is an Arduino Nano:

Arduino Leonardo

Arduino Leonardo is similar to Arduino Uno. The main difference is that it has a soldered microcontroller instead of a removable one, and the model of the microcontroller is ATmega32U4. It has 20 digital pins and 12 analog inputs. The following image is an Arduino Leonardo with the ATmega32U4 microcontroller's pin out:

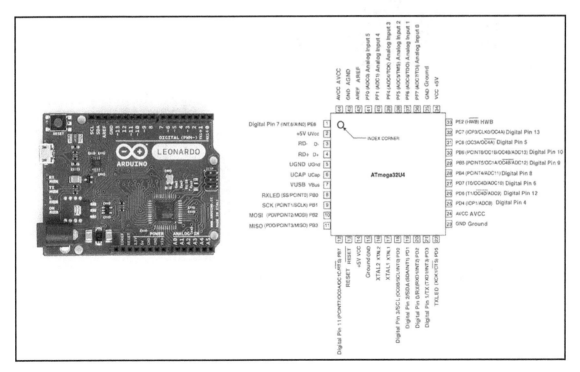

Arduino Mini

Arduino Mini is a small prototyping device that is based on the ATmega168. It does not come with a USB port. Arduino Mini has 14 digital pins and eight analog inputs. The ATmega168 has 16Kbytes of flash memory, 20MHz maximum operating frequency and an 8-bit AVR CPU. The following image is an Arduino Mini and an ATmega168 microcontroller with its pin out. The following image is image of an Arduino menu with the ATmega168's pin out:

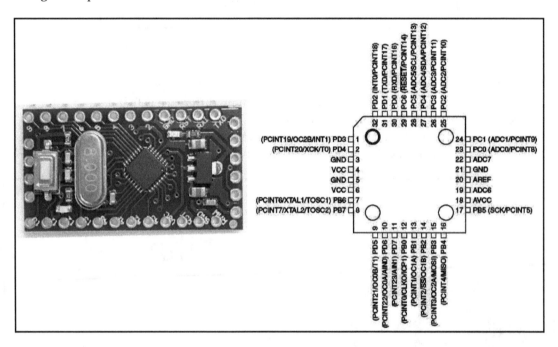

Arduino Micro

Arduino Micro is based on the ATmega32u4 microcontroller. It uses the same microcontroller as the Arduino Leonardo. There are fewer digital and analog pins than in the Arduino Leonardo – the Micro has 20 digital pins. It comes with a micro USB port and ICSP pins. The following image is an Arduino Micro:

Throughout this book, we will use the most famous board, Arduino Uno. Arduino Uno has a replaceable microcontroller, ATmega 328. Before connecting an Arduino to our PC, let's get to know our Arduino better.

Exploring Arduino Uno

An Arduino Uno consists of a number of parts. The important ones are as follows:

- USB port
- External power supply port
- Analog pins
- Digital pins
- ICSP
- Microcontroller
- Reset button

Let's know about them in detail.

USB port

This port is used to power up the Arduino board and upload programs into the microcontroller:

On the Arduino Uno, the USB port is situated in between the reset button and the voltage regulator.

A-B cable is needed for powering up the board and uploading code to the microcontroller. The following picture is an A-B cable:

The 'A' side is connected to the Arduino board and the 'B' side is connected to the USB port of the computer.

External power jack

Via this port, we can power the Arduino, but we cannot upload a program using it. This port is usually a 7-12 volt DC input. The following picture is a spare port and an adapter of 7-12 volts. The following picture is an external power jack and a port of 3.5mm power:

Analog pins

On an Arduino Uno, there are six analog pins (**A0**, **A1**, **A2**, **A3**, **A4** and **A5**). The analog pins are used for reading analog values. We will discuss the uses of the analog pins in the next chapter.

The following image shows the analog inputs of the Arduino Uno:

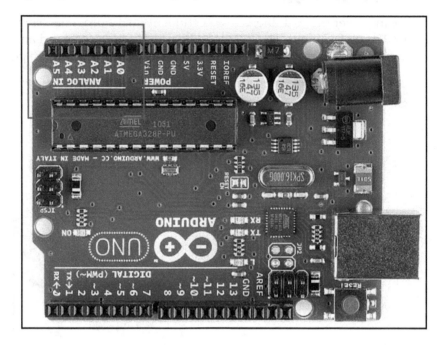

Digital pins

On an Arduino Uno there are 14 digital pins (0-13). The digital pins are used for reading digital values from sensors, generating digital signals and communicating with other devices through digital interfaces. The following image shows the position of the digital pins of the Arduino Uno:

ICSP

There are two sets of **ICSP (In Circuit Serial Programming)** pins on an Arduino Uno board. On the image below, you can see both of them (A and B). These ICSP pins are used for updating the firmware or reinstalling the bootloader, which is something you should not worry about in this book:

Firmware is permanent software that is programmed on the read-only memory, and bootloader is a computer program that helps to load the operating system.

Microcontroller

There is a main microcontroller on our Arduino. By microcontroller we mean a single computer or a collection of processor core, memory and input/output peripherals. On our Arduino Uno we have ATmega328. Let's see the pin out of the microcontroller:

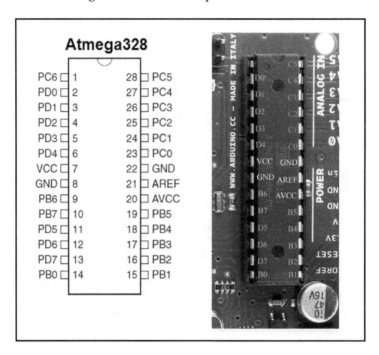

The pins are defined as follows:

Pin number	Pin name on the microcontroller	Pin name on Arduino
1	PC6	Reset
2	PD0	0 (RX)
3	PD1	1 (TX)
4	PD2	2
5	PD3	3 (PWM)
6	PD4	4
7	VCC	VCC
8	GND	GND

9	PB6	Crystal
10	PB7	Crystal
11	PD5	5 (PWM)
12	PD6	6 (PWM)
13	PD7	7
14	PB0	8
15	PB1	9 (PWM)
16	PB2	10 (PWM)
17	PB3	11 (PWM)
18	PB4	12
19	PB5	13
20	AVCC	VCC
21	AREF	AREF
22	GND	GND
23	PC0	A0
24	PC1	A1
25	PC2	A2
26	PC3	A3
27	PC4	A4
28	PC5	A5

 PWM means **Pulse Width Modulation**. This is a process by which we get analog results by digital means. GND is Ground, and VCC is the power (3.5V or 5V).

Reset button

On Arduino Uno there is a reset button between the USB port and the digital pins. The following pins show a reset button of Arduino Uno. This button is used to refresh the board or restart the system:

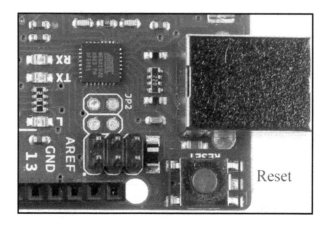

Now we know all we need about Arduino Uno, let's connect it to the computer and program for our Arduino Uno.

Connecting Arduino to PC

To connect Arduino Uno to our system we will need an A-B cable, about which we have already learned. Let's connect the Arduino as shown in the following image:

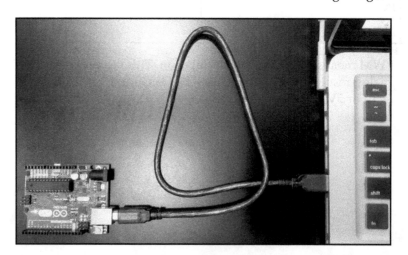

You will hear a sound on your system after connecting the Arduino Uno to the PC. A green light on the Arduino Uno will glow. If the green light does not glow, something went wrong. You need to check the connection or see Chapter 10, *Few Error Handlings*:

Now, we will download the IDE for coding for the Arduino and uploading to the board.

Downloading and installing Arduino IDE

Arduino IDE is an Integrated Development Environment where we can write code, debug and upload to our Arduino Uno or any other board.

Downloading Arduino IDE

To download Arduino IDE, we need to go to `https://www.arduino.cc/en/Main/Software` and you will see the following page:

We will download the package associated with our Operating System.

Installing Arduino IDE

Let's install Arduino IDE on our system.

Installing Arduino IDE on Windows

To install Arduino IDE on Windows, go to the previous link and download **Windows Installer** or **Windows Zip file for non admin install.** I would recommend you choose the installer file because the other file is a portable IDE, which may show errors with the drivers of the Arduino.

You will see the following page after clicking on any of the files:

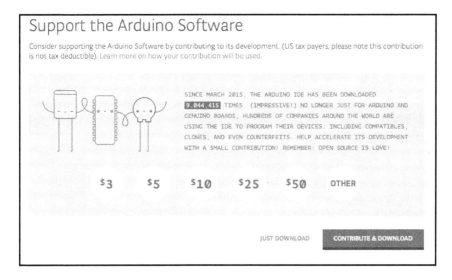

You may Contribute and Download or Just Download.

After downloading the **Windows Installer** file, you will have an `.exe` file. Double click on the file to get started. I would recommend right clicking on the `.exe` file and selecting **Run as Administrator,** as shown in the image below:

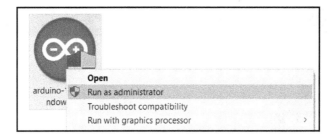

The rest of the processes are similar to an ordinary installation.

Installing Arduino IDE on Ubuntu/Linux

On most modern Linux distributions you can download the **Linux 32 bits or Linux 64 bits** depending on your system architecture.

On Ubuntu and most Debian-based distributions you can use the command line to download and install the IDE from official package sources. Open your terminal (*Ctrl+Alt+T*) and write the following line and press *Enter*.

```
sudo apt-get install arduino arduino-core
```

You will be prompted to enter your password. Enter your password and hit *Enter*:

```
Towaha:~/Desktop/Learning C for Arduino> sudo apt-get install Arduino
[sudo] password for soft:
Reading package lists... Done
Building dependency tree
Reading state information... Done
E: Unable to locate package Arduino
Towaha:~/Desktop/Learning C for Arduino> sudo apt-get install Arduino-ide
Reading package lists... Done
Building dependency tree
Reading state information... Done
Towaha:~/Desktop/Learning C for Arduino> sudo apt-get install arduino arduino-core
```

You will be shown the following message on your terminal. Type Y and hit *Enter*:

```
Building dependency tree
Reading state information... Done
E: Unable to locate package Arduino
Towaha:~/Desktop/Learning C for Arduino> sudo apt-get install Arduino-ide
Reading package lists... Done
Building dependency tree
Reading state information... Done
Towaha:~/Desktop/Learning C for Arduino> sudo apt-get install arduino arduino-core
Reading package lists... Done
Building dependency tree
Reading state information... Done
The following additional packages will be installed:
  avr-libc avrdude binutils-avr extra-xdg-menus gcc-avr libftdi1 libjna-java libjna-jni
  librxtx-java
Suggested packages:
  arduino-mk avrdude-doc task-c-devel gcc-doc libjna-java-doc
The following NEW packages will be installed:
  arduino arduino-core avr-libc avrdude binutils-avr extra-xdg-menus gcc-avr libftdi1
  libjna-java libjna-jni librxtx-java
0 upgraded, 11 newly installed, 0 to remove and 5 not upgraded.
Need to get 20.9 MB of archives.
After this operation, 123 MB of additional disk space will be used.
Do you want to continue? [Y/n]
```

If no error occurs, you will see the following screen:

```
Terminal
File Edit View Search Terminal Help
Processing 2 added doc-base files...
Processing triggers for man-db (2.7.5-1) ...
Processing triggers for libc-bin (2.23-0ubuntu3) ...
Processing triggers for bamfdaemon (0.5.3~bzr0+16.04.20160701-0ubuntu1) ...
Rebuilding /usr/share/applications/bamf-2.index...
Processing triggers for gnome-menus (3.13.3-6ubuntu3.1) ...
Processing triggers for desktop-file-utils (0.22-1ubuntu5) ...
Processing triggers for mime-support (3.59ubuntu1) ...
Processing triggers for hicolor-icon-theme (0.15-0ubuntu1) ...
Processing triggers for shared-mime-info (1.5-2ubuntu0.1) ...
Setting up libjna-jni (4.2.2-1) ...
Setting up libjna-java (4.2.2-1) ...
Setting up librxtx-java (2.2pre2-13) ...
Setting up binutils-avr (2.25+Atmel3.5.0-2) ...
Setting up gcc-avr (1:4.9.2+Atmel3.5.0-1) ...
Setting up libftdi1:amd64 (0.20-4build1) ...
Setting up avrdude (6.2-5) ...
Setting up avr-libc (1:1.8.0+Atmel3.5.0-1) ...
Setting up arduino-core (2:1.0.5+dfsg2-4) ...
Setting up arduino (2:1.0.5+dfsg2-4) ...
Setting up extra-xdg-menus (1.0-4) ...
Processing triggers for libc-bin (2.23-0ubuntu3) ...
Towaha:~/Desktop/Learning C for Arduino>
```

Installing Arduino IDE on Mac

To install Arduino IDE for mac, download the **Mac OS X 10.7 Lion or newer** file. You will see the `Arduino.app` file in your download folder. Double click on the file and you will first see a message that says verifying the `Arduino.app`. Then you will see a warning as the following image:

Click **Open** to open the Arduino IDE.

You may not see the option **Open.** All you need is to press the `Control/Option` Key of your mac and click on the `Arduino.app` file, and you will see the **Open** option.

You may copy the `Arduino.app` file into your `Application` folder for frequent access.

Explore Arduino IDE

Now we have downloaded and installed the Arduino IDE on our system, let's explore the IDE.

In Windows, just open the installed Arduino software. On Ubuntu/Linux, type the following line in the terminal and hit *Enter*:

```
sudo Arduino
```

On the mac, just open the `Arduino.app` file.

No matter which operating system you use, you will see almost the following screen on every platform:

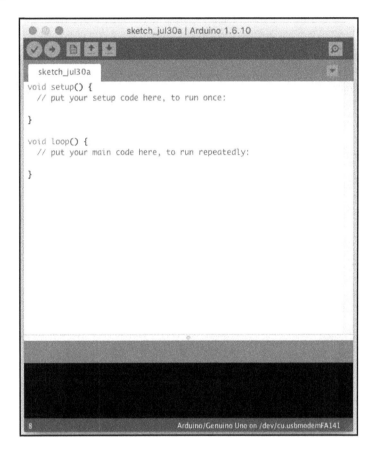

At the top of the screen you will find all the menus for the Arduino Uno. Before learning anything, let's configure our Arduino Uno with the Arduino IDE. We have already connected our Arduino to our PC via an A-B cable. Now, from the menu, go to **Tools** | **Board** and select Arduino Uno. Then go to port and select the port on which the Arduino is connected:

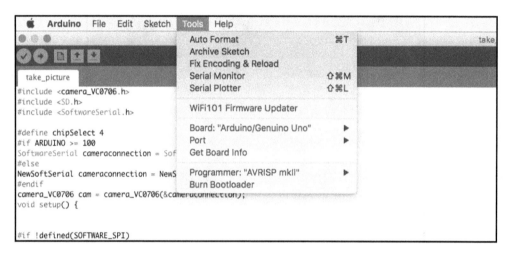

If you find difficulty in selecting the port, please have a look at Chapter 10, *Few Error Handlings*.

If everything looks good, then we are now ready to write code for Arduino and upload it to the board.

Let's explore all the menus and their functions. In the **File** menu you will see the following options:

- **New**: Thisoption enables you to create a new Arduino file.
- **Open**: This option opens an existing Arduino file.
- **Open Recent**: This shows the recent Arduino files.
- **Sketchbook**: This shows the stored files.
- **Examples**: This shows the common Arduino Programs and other library file-related examples.
- **Close**: This option closes the Arduino tab.
- **Save**: This option saves the Arduino code you want to save inside a folder and adds an `.ino` extension to the file.
- **Save as**: This allows you to save the file as other formats (for example a text file).
- **Page Setup**: This option helps to set up the print screen of the code.

- **Print** options let you print the code.
- **Preference**: This shows the following screen, where you can customize the look of your Arduino IDE, for example the location of your sketchbooks, size of fonts, type of fonts, display line numbers and so on. I would suggest checking the Display.

Line numbers option for the debugging suitability:

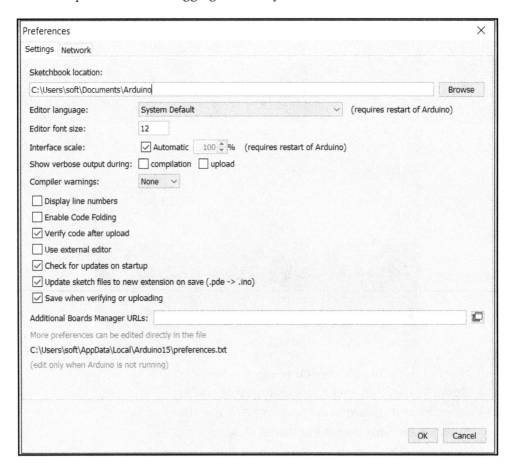

- **Quit** option helps to exit the Arduino IDE at any time
- The **Edit** option shows the following screen:

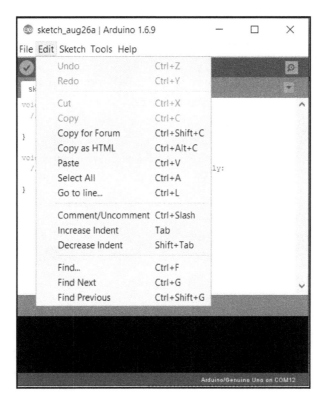

In the **Edit** menu, you will see the following options:

- **Undo**: This option allows you to undo any error in the code or go back to the previous step of the code.
- **Redo**: This option allows you to go forward if you have selected undo before.
- **Cut**: This option cuts the line of code.
- **Copy**: This option copies the selected text.
- **Copy for Forum**: This formats code for the Arduino forum.
- *** Copy as HTML**: This copies code as an HTML document. This option is used to publish the Arduino code to the web. It's an option that allows you to export the code in a web format (using HTML, CSS etc). Just click this option after writing the code, and your code will be copied as the web format. You can then use it in an HTML file.
- **Paste**: This option allows you to paste the copied text.

- **Select All**: This selects all the code.
- **Go to line**: This allows you to go to the desired line.
- **Comment/Uncomment**: This allows you to comment or uncomment any text on the code.
- **IncreaseIndent**: This moves code to the right using spaces (organizes code for better readability).
- **DecreaseIndent**: This moves code to the left, removing spaces.
- **Find**: This helps to find any text in the text editor.
- **FindNext**: This helps you to find the next keyword when searching in the text editor.
- **FindPrevious**: This helps you to find the previous keyword that was searched for in the text editor:

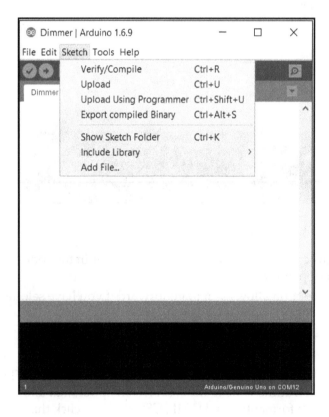

In the **Sketch** menu you will see the following options:

- **Verify/Compile**: This option compiles the code we write in the text editor into machine code for the Arduino microcontroller. In doing so, it also verifies the code to find any programming errors.
- **Upload:** This option helps to upload the code we write in the text editor to the Arduino board.
- **Upload Using programmer**: In the Arduino Uno, we use an ATmega328 microcontroller. By default, when we purchase it, it comes preinstalled with a tiny program known as a bootloader, and using this we can upload code to the board directly. If there was no bootloader, we would need an external programmer to upload code to the Arduino. So, if we need to change the removable microcontroller for a new one, it might not contain the bootloader pre-installed. For this reason, we use this option. We connect the Arduino with a fresh microcontroller and another old Arduino with a pre-installed bootloader. Then we upload to the new one using the old one as a programmer.
- **Export compiled binary**: We sometimes need .hex files for microcontrollers. This option allows us to convert the Arduino code into hex format.

Hex file is a file format that conveys binary data into ASCII text format.

- **Show Sketch Folder**: This folder shows the directory of the sketch files we save.
- **Include Library**: There are a number of libraries for Arduino, about which we will learn more in Chapter 8, *Working with Arduino Libraries*. Using this option, we can add libraries to our code. All we need to do is just select a library and the Arduino application will automatically add the library to the code.

- **Add File...** By using this option, we can add files (any file) to our sketch folder:

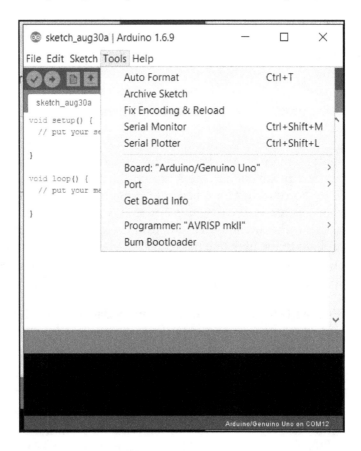

In the **Tools** menu, you will see the following options:

- **Auto Format**: We sometime do not maintain clean code. The code might not be understood by others if we do so. This option auto formats the whole code and makes it readable.
- **Archive Sketch**: To make a zip folder that includes all the sketch files inside our sketch folder, we use this option.
- **Fix Encoding and Reload**: This fixes the character encoding of the text file and reloads it.

- **Serial Monitor**: This is one of the most useful options of the Arduino application. With this option we can monitor the data input/output on the Arduino. We will discuss this option later.
- **Serial Plotter**: With this option we can also monitor the serial, but visually. We can create graphs using this option. You will be given examples of the serial plotter later.
- **Board**: Using this option you can select your Arduino board, which is connected to your PC.
- **Port**: With this option, we can select the port to which our Arduino is connected.
- **Get Board Info**: This option shows the Arduino board information, which is connected to the PC.
- * **Programmer**: This option selects the programmer if we want to burn our microcontroller or burn a bootloader on another Arduino. By default, AVRISP mkll is selected.
- **Burn Bootloader**: This option helps to burn the bootloader on another Arduino.

Summary

In this first chapter we have learned all the basic information about an Arduino, especially Arduino Uno. Don't worry about other types of Arduino, because they have almost the same functionalities. Sometimes the number of pins is greater, or the microcontroller is faster (and so on) on other types of Arduino.

I would suggest you read the whole chapter and get to know your Arduino better for the following chapters. If you want to learn only C programming, not for Arduino, then you can skip this chapter.

2
Our First Program!

In this chapter, we will be learning how to connect our **Arduino** to our system and make it ready for uploading our very first C program with Arduino IDE.

Let's get started. I am assuming you have got your own Arduino Uno and an A-B cable to connect it to your PC. If you haven't, I recommend you pick up an Arduino Uno (any version will do, but Arduino Uno is preferred) and follow this chapter. You can buy Arduinos from any electronics shop or order online. You can go to `https://www.arduino.c` `c/en/Main/buy` to find a store in your locality to buy an Arduino.

Connecting your Arduino

In the previous chapter, we learned how to connect an Arduino to our system. Let's do it again.

First, connect your A-B cable to your PC, and then connect the cable to the board. Your PC will make a sound to confirm that the Arduino has connected to the PC, and the on-board on/off LED will turn on.

Now open the Arduino IDE. From the menu, go to **Tools** ∣ **Board** ∣ **Arduino/Genuino Uno**. You can select any board you have bought from the list. See the following screenshot for the list:

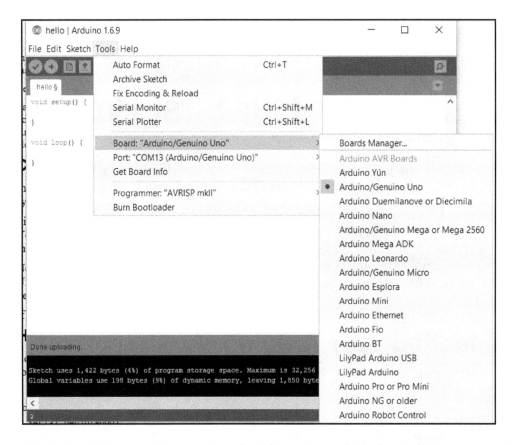

Now let's do the tricky part. You have to select the port on which the Arduino is connected. There are a lot of things you can do to find out. We will discuss few of them in Chapter 10, *Few Error Handlings*. If you have the latest version of Arduino IDE and go to **Tools** ∣ **Port**, and you will see a bunch of port lists, but on the port on which your Arduino is connected, you will see something similar to the following. In my case, it is port number COM13 (on Windows). Select the port beside which your connected board name is written (on Linux and OSX):

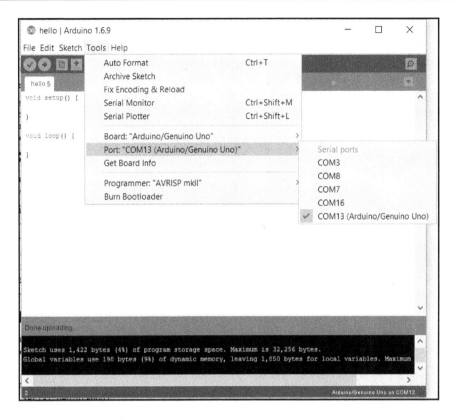

Keep everything unchanged.

If there are any errors, please refer to Chapter 10, *Few Error Handlings*.

Hello Arduino!

Let's write our first program on the Arduino IDE. Go to **File** and click **New**. A text editor will open with a few lines of code. Delete those lines first. Then, on the editor section, type the following code. Don't worry, the code will be explained later:

```
void setup() {
  Serial.begin(9600);
}

void loop() {
  Serial.print("Hello Arduino!\n");
}
```

From the menu, go to **Sketch** and click **Upload**. It is a good practice to verify/compile the code before uploading it to the Arduino board. There will be a prompt to save the code on your system. Just give it any name you want and save it. To verify/compile the code, you need to go to **Sketch** and click **Verify/Compile**. You will see the message **DoneCompiling** on the bottom of the IDE if the code is error-free. See the following screenshot:

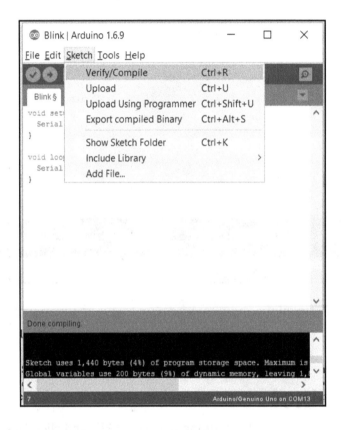

After the successful upload, you need to open the Serial Monitor of the Arduino IDE. To open the Serial Monitor, you need to go to **Tools** and click **SerialMonitor**. You will see the following screen:

Dissecting our first code

Now let's discuss how the code compiled on the board and the structure of the code.

The basic structure of the code is as follows:

```
void setup() {

}

void loop() {

}
```

There are two functions in our code. The `setup()` function and the `loop()` function. Every Arduino code will have these two functions. Let's get to the functions better.

setup() function

The `setup()` function helps to initialize variables and set pin modes, and we can also use libraries here. This function is called first when we compile/upload the whole code. `setup()` runs only for the first time it is uploaded to the board and later, it runs every time we press the Reset button on the Arduino.

In our code, we used `Serial.begin(9600)`, which sets the data rate per second for the serial communication. We know that serial communication is the process by which we send data one bit at a time over a communication channel. For Arduino to communicate with the computer, we used the data rate 9600, which is a standard data rate.

This is also known as baud rate. We can set the baud rate any of the following, depending on the connection speed and type:

- 300
- 1200
- 2400
- 4800
- 9600
- 19200
- 38400
- 57600
- 74880
- 115200
- 230400
- 250000

I will recommend using 9600 for general data-communication purposes. If you use a higher baud rate, the characters we print might be broken, because our Arduino might not be speedy enough to process the bits at a higher baud rate.

If we do not declare the baud rate inside the `setup()` function, there will be no output on the serial monitor.

Baud rate 9600 means 960 characters per second. This is because, in serial communication, you need to transmit one start bit, eight data bits, and one stop bit, for a total of 10 bits at a speed of 9600 bits per second.

loop() function

The `loop()` function will let the code run again and again, until we disconnect the Arduino from the power source.

We have written a print statement inside the `loop()` function, which will execute infinitely. To print something on the serial monitor, we need to write the following line:

```
Serial.print("Anything We Want To Print");
```

Between the quotations, we can write anything we want to print. In the preceding code, we have written `Serial.print("Hello Arduino!\n")`. That's why, on the serial monitor, we saw that **Hello Arduino!** was printing infinitely. We used \n after **Hello Arduino!** This is called the escape sequence. For now, just remember we need to put this after each line inside the print statement to break a line and print the next command on the next line. We will learn more about the escape sequence in Chapter 3, *Exploring C with Arduino*.

We can use `Serial.println("Hello Arduino!");` instead of `Serial.print("Hello Arduino!\n");`. Both will give the same result.

Now, what do we need to do if we want to print *Hello Arduino!* only once?

Yes, you are right. We need to put `Serial.println("Hello Arduino!")` inside the `setup()` function. Now let's see what happens if we put a print statement inside the `setup()` function. Have a look at the following screenshot. *Hello Arduino!* is printed only once:

Things to remember

The following sections cover some things you need to remember.

Watch your case

C is case sensitive. So, we need to take care about what we type, or our code won't compile. For example, `loop()` and `Loop()` are not the same thing in C. We cannot use `serial.print("Hello Arduino!");` instead of `Serial.print("Hello Arduino!");`.

Don't forget your semicolon!

Now look at the following code. Can you tell where it went wrong?

```
void setup() {
 Serial.begin(9600)
 Serial.println("Arduino is fun");
}
void loop() {
}
```

Exactly! On the second line, we missed a semicolon. Let's see if our Arduino IDE can detect the error. We wrote the code in the editor of our Arduino IDE and clicked the verify button (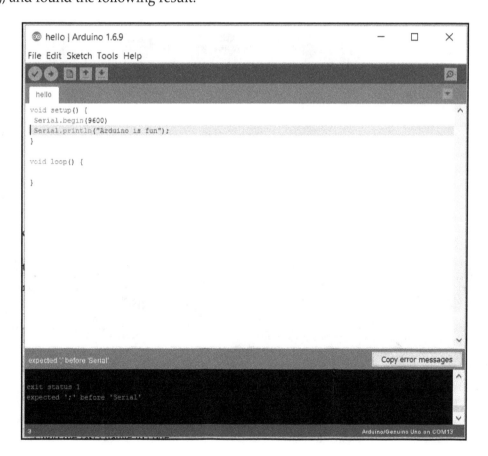), and found the following result:

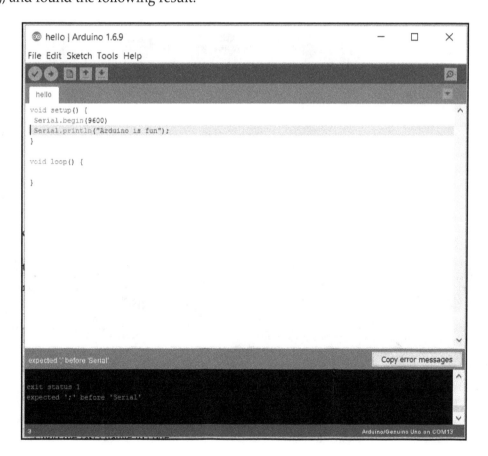

From this screen, we can see that our Arduino IDE could detect the error. The log (the black portion of the Arduino IDE) shows where the error occurred. The log says, *expected ';' before 'Serial'*, which means we missed a semicolon before `Serial.println("Arduino is fun");`.

Adding both Setup() and Loop() functions

You cannot forget to add either the `setup()` function or the `loop()` function to our code. They must be added to the code. Say we forgot to add the `loop()` function. We will see the following error. The same error will occur if we miss the `setup()` function:

Minding the baud rate

Say I have added `Serial.begin(9600)` to our `setup` function. Our code will be as follows:

```
void setup() {
 Serial.begin(9600);
 Serial.println("Today");
 Serial.println("is");
 Serial.println("a");
 Serial.println("wonderful");
 Serial.println("day!");
}

void loop() {
}
```

Clearly, the output of the code on the serial monitor will be as follows:

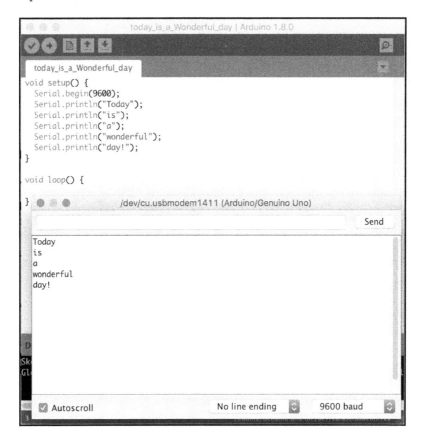

But if, on the serial monitor, we accidentally change the baud rate to something else, say, 19200, what will happen? What will the output on the serial monitor be? The output will be similar to the following screenshot:

So, we need to have a look at the baud rate. If you are not doing any high-speed communication keep both the baud rates at 9600.

Formatting your code

Take a look at the following images. Which code is more readable, left or right?

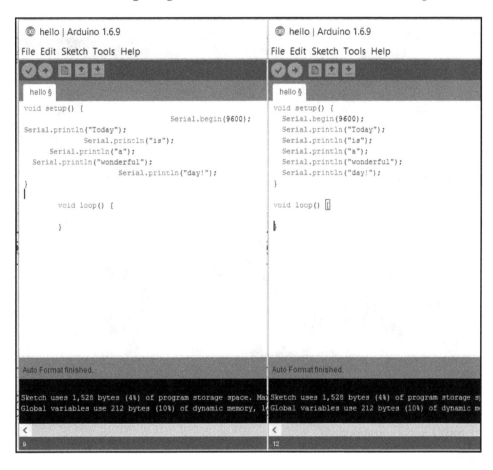

The code on the right is more readable because it clear-coded. So, it is necessary to format our code. We can do it manually. On Arduino IDE, you can format your code automatically, too. To do this automatically, we need to go to **Tools** and select **Auto Format**. Your code will be formatted as the code on the right-hand side of the preceding image.

Turning the LED On

If you have a closer look at your Arduino Uno, you will see a few LEDs integrated to the board. See the following figure for a better look:

There are four LEDs on the board:

- LED on pin 13 (connected with Arduino pin 13)
- Power LED (turns on when the Arduino is powered)
- Rx and Tx LEDs (turn on when Arduino code is uploaded or data is transferred via 0 and 1 Arduino pins)

We can program the LED connected with pin 13. After we upload any code to our board, usually, the LED on pin 13 turns on.

Now we will write code to control the LED. You can also connect an external LED on pin 13, and a ground pin with a proper resistor, as shown in the following figure. If you have an external LED connected to the board, it will be clear to you if the LED is being controlled by the code, since the integrated LED is small:

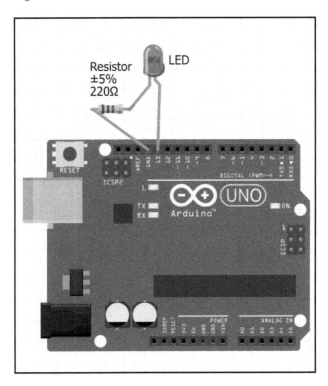

 The positive leg of the LED will go to pin 13 of the Arduino, and the negative leg will connect to one end of the resistor; the other end of the resistor will go to any of the ground pins on the Arduino. Usually, the longer leg of the LED is positive and the shorter leg is negative. Another way to find out the positive and negative leg is to look through the LED; you will see a flat plate and a sharp plate. The outer part of the sharp plate is positive, and the flat plate's outer leg is negative.

Now let's write our code to turn the LED on. Write the following code in the Arduino text editor, creating a new file on the Arduino Uno:

```
void setup() {
  pinMode(13, OUTPUT);
}
```

```
void loop() {
}
```

We know that the `setup()` function holds the variables. In the preceding code, we have written a `pinMode()` function, where we have passed two parameters: the pin number, and the result of pinMode. `pinMode(13, OUTPUT);` means we have selected pin 13. So, we can now control anything connected to pin 13.

The `pinMode()` function is for the digital pins of the Arduino board. If you are not sure about the digital pins of the Arduino board, please refer back to `Chapter 1`, *Getting Started*

If you want to use any other pins (say, pins 9, 6, 4, and 3), can you guess what you have to write?

Exactly. The `pinMode` of the pins will be as follows:

```
pinMode(9, OUTPUT);
pinMode(6, OUTPUT);
pinMode(4, OUTPUT);
pinMode(3, OUTPUT);
```

Be careful to write *OUTPUT* in all capital letters.

Now we will send a signal to pin 13 to turn the LED on. There are two kinds of signals, *LOW* and *HIGH*. *LOW* is for sending no signal to the pin, and *HIGH* is for sending a signal to the pin. You can use 0 and 1 instead of *LOW* and *HIGH*.

Let's send a HIGH signal to pin 13. Since pin 13 is a digital pin, we need to send the signal using the following function:

```
digitalWrite(13, HIGH);
```

The `digitalWrite()` function has two parameters; the first one is pin number and the second one is the pulse, or signal. It works for only digital pins. Remember that you cannot use the pin number on this function if you do not write the `pinMode()` function with the same pin number. To use a digital pin and give it a signal (either HIGH or LOW), you must write two functions to declare and use the pin. The `pinMode()` function is used to declare the pin that we have connected something to, and the `digitalWrite()` function allows us to send a signal to the defined pin.

If we want to send no signal to the pin 13, we need to write the following function:

```
digitalWrite(13, LOW);
```

We can use 0 and 1 instead of *LOW* and *HIGH.* So, we can write digitalWrite(13, 1) and digitalWrite(13,0) instead of digitalWrite(13, HIGH) and digitalWrite(13, LOW), respectively.

What should we do if we want to turn the LED on? I guess you know that already.

Yes, we need to write the digitalWrite() function inside the setup() function, unless we do not want to send the same signal again and again.

So, the code to turn on the LED on pin 13 will be as follows:

```
void setup() {
  pinMode(13, OUTPUT);
  digitalWrite(13, HIGH);//Sends a pulse to pin 13
}

void loop() {

}
```

If you upload the code to the board, you will see that the LED is turned on. Let's turn it off now. You can easily guess what the code to turn our LED off will be, right?

It is as follows:

```
void setup() {
  pinMode(13, OUTPUT);
  digitalWrite(13, LOW); //Sends no pulse to pin 13
}

void loop() {

}
```

Have you noticed that we can switch our LED on or off from our code without even touching the LED? Isn't it exciting? How about we make it more interesting: let's blink our LED!

Blink a LED

To blink a LED, we need to know about time. I am sure you are asking yourself what should you know about time. Think about blinking a LED. You will see there is a delay between the LED turning and off, right? And it needs to be done repeatedly. Am I thinking the right things? Yes! So, first we need to turn the LED on, then we make a delay, then turn the LED off, and make a delay again. Then repeat the whole thing again. So, what is the algorithm for the blinking LED? Let's see:

1. Turn the LED on, SET the pin HIGH.
2. Delay sometimes depends on how quickly the blinking will happen.
3. Turn the LED off, SET the pin LOW.
4. Repeat step 2.
5. Repeat steps 1 to 4.

Now you can easily envision how the blinking happens. Let's write our blinking code now. But, before we write the code, let me introduce you to another function, called `delay()`. This will handle the waiting between the LED turning on and off. This means this function will stop or hold off on sending signals to the board for a defined time passed inside the function. Inside our `delay()` function, we will pass the time in milliseconds. Say we want to wait one second in between turning the LED on and off; we need to write the following:

```
delay(1000);
```

 1,000 milliseconds = 1 second. So, we need to multiply the time in seconds by 1,000, inside the `delay()` function, to get the correct time.

According to our algorithm, the code for blinking will be as follows. We need to write the blinking part of the code inside the `loop()` function. Can you guess why? Yes! To make the blinking repeat. The code is as follows:

```
void setup() {
  pinMode(13, OUTPUT);
  digitalWrite(13, HIGH); // you may delete this line, do you know why?
}

void loop() {
  digitalWrite(13, HIGH);
  delay(1000);
  digitalWrite(13, LOW);
  delay(1000);
}
```

You can see that we have made pin 13 high, which turns the LED on; then we had a delay of one second and turned the LED off, and again had a delay of one second.

The whole thing runs again and again as we have written the pulse sending part to the pin 13 inside the `loop()` function. Let's upload the code and look at the result:

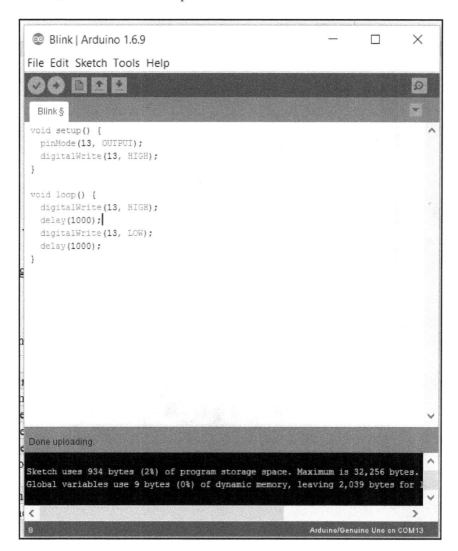

Yes! Our LED is blinking with a one-second delay!

Commenting

Imagine one of your friends knows how to use and programme an Arduino. He wrote some code and e-mailed you. You know a little programming. Let's imagine he e-mailed the following code:

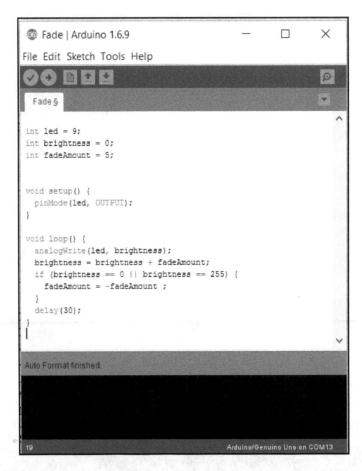

From the code, you can understand only the setup() and delay() functions, as we just learned about them a moment ago.

What happens in the rest of the code? Isn't it totally new to you? If your friend had sent you the following code, would not you understand more?

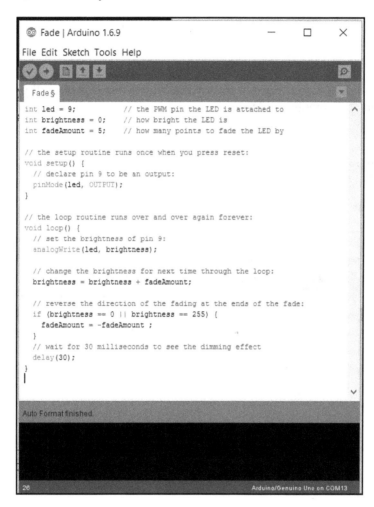

Yes! You can now understand the code a little bit more, right? Why? Because, written in the code is what happens for each of the lines. See that?

In programming, this is known as commenting. It is a good practice to comment on any code that's a little harder for you. You might not remember what you did on a specific line; the commenting will help in that case.

So, how should you write your comment? It is simple. For a single-line comment, you just place two forward slashes before the comment, as follows:

```
//I am a comment
//I will help you to understand the code
//I cannot be read by the compiler: D
//I am invisible to the compiler: D
```

For a multi-line comment, you need to follow the following example. All you need to do is place all your long comments inside /* and */:

```
/* I am a comment
I will help you to understand the code
I cannot be read by the compiler: D
I am invisible to the compiler: D */
```

Let's look at how it will appear in the editor:

You can see that the comments are in gray. The compiler cannot read the comments; only humans can.

Try at home

How about you try the following things at home? Don't worry, they will be explained later:

1. Try to understand the code your friend sent you via e-mail.
2. Connect an external LED to your Arduino and play with it by changing the values of the `delay()` function.
3. Upload the code to your board and look at the result. (You might need an external LED for the code-the integrated LED might not work properly.)

Sometimes, we need to work quickly; if you know the keyboard shortcuts, the task becomes much easier.

Keyboard shortcuts

Let's look at a few keyboard shortcuts for Arduino IDE, which will help you to work way faster:

Windows/Linux	Mac OS	Action
Ctrl +N	Command +N	Open a new sketch.
Ctrl +O	Command +O	Open an existing sketch.
Ctrl +S	Command +S	Save the sketch.
Ctrl +Shift+S	Command +Shift+S	Save the sketch with a new name.

Ctrl +R	Command +R	Compile/Verify a sketch.
Ctrl +T	Command +T	Auto Format. Adjusts the alignment and spacing of your code.
Ctrl +Z	Command +Z	Undo the last change to your code.
Ctrl +Shift+Z	Command +Shift+Z	Redo the last change to your code.
Ctrl +/	Command +/	Comment/uncomment selected code.
Ctrl +U	Command +U	Upload the sketch to the Arduino board.
Ctrl +Shift+M	Command +Shift+M	Open the serial monitor.

Summary

In this chapter, we have learned how to connect the Arduino to our system and how to verify/compile the code. We then uploaded some sample code to our board. We have learned how the Arduino code works. We also learned how to play with an LED. We made the LED blink indefinitely. I would suggest you change the delay time and play with the blinking code. Who knows, you might find something interesting or invent a Morse-code generator!

3
Exploring C with Arduino IDE

In the last chapter, we learned about basic Arduino coding. We also played with LEDs using an Arduino, by programming the microcontroller through the **Arduino IDE**. In this chapter, we are going to learn more about the C programming used for coding in Arduino IDE. We will also go deeper into C and some simple circuits in this chapter. We will learn about the data types of C, how we can declare our variables in C, how we can take an input and print in C, some mathematical operations, arrays, and strings. Let's start our journey into exploring C programming with Arduino IDE.

Variables

Variables are used to store data in programming languages. You might remember from your algebra class that, *The number of chocolates is x,* where we didn't know the value of x, but after the math was done, we found the value of x. Let's make it clear by giving an example. Consider a scenario: *A boy has 23 pencils; he buys 13 pencils. How many pencils does he have now?*

It's simple. Just sum up all the numbers. But let's try to do it using a variable. We can solve it as follows:

The number of pencils the boy has now is x:

So, x = 23+13 Or, x = 46

We have found the value of x, which is the total number of pencils the boy has now.

Have you noticed we stored the number of pencils on the variable x? Yes, this is what we do with variables.

In C programming, we often need to declare variables inside our code. During the C program execution, an entity that may vary is called a variable. There are a few rules for declaring a variable name. We cannot name our variables however we want, but aside from the following rules, we can use any variable name we want. The rules are:

You cannot declare a variable that starts with a number. For example, *1stNumber, 007User, 2ndName*, and so on cannot be declared as variables in C.

Your variable's name should not contain any symbols. This means that *&name, %testVar, #time*, and so on cannot be declared and used in C programming as variable names. That said, the dollar sign ($) and underscore (_) are fine to be used in a variable name. However, in Arduino IDE, we cannot use a dollar sign ($) in the variable name. This will show error.

Your variables must not have blank spaces, which means, *my test, his name, the cost* , and so on are not valid variables in C.

The variables cannot contain commas or periods. *My.variable, my, age* , and so on are not valid.

Other than the preceding rules, you should also remember that your variable name can have up to 247 characters. On some compilers, it is limited to 31 characters. Since C programming is case sensitive, *myname* and *MYNAME* are different variables.

Exercise

Can you tell me which of the following variable names is valid and why?

_number, $name, varItems, 0isScore, -number, look@me, ~var, TimeLimit, my1stclass, weeknumber1, december23, 23october, like+ride.

Aside from the rules and length limit of a variable name, there is one thing we should remember. We cannot use reserved keywords as our variable names. There are a few reserved keywords in C that we cannot use for declaring variables. The reserved keywords are:
auto, break, case, char, const, continue, default, do, double, else, enum, extern, float, for, goto, if, int, long, register, return, short, signed, sizeof, static, struct, switch, typeof, union, unsigned, void, volatile, while.

Data types

In our day-to-day life, we use numbers, alphabets, words, and sentences. These can be defined as data. Again, numbers can be divided into two types: fraction and non-fraction, or integer and non-integer. Alphabets and symbols can be defined as characters. Let's look at what we call them in C, and their memory allocation. I will explain what memory allocation is and how you can find out how much memory a data type is consuming later.

Integers

Numbers that can be written without a fractional part are called **integers:** 5, 28, 273, 100, 986,343 are integers. There are negative integers too: -56, -87, -23,453, -1,000, and so on. They are called *int* in C programming. If we want to set a variable (*number*) equal to an integer (here, 24) we can write the following:

```
int number = 24;
```

An integer occupies 2 bytes (16 bits) or 4 bytes (32 bits) of memory depending on the processor's architecture. On 32-bit computers, an integer occupies 2 bytes of memory, and on 64-bit computers, integer occupies 4 bytes of memory. For an Arduino Uno, an integer is 2 bytes. A 2-byte integer can hold a number between 2^{-15} to 2^{15}-1 (-32,768 to 32,767). A 4-byte integer can hold a number between 2^{-31} to 2^{31}-1 (-2,147,483,648 to 2,147,483,647). If a longer number is needed there is another data type in C, named *long int* or *long long int*, which can hold longer numbers.

Rational numbers or fractions

In C programming, there are two types of rational numbers. We call them *float* or *double*. A *float* usually occupies shorter memory than a *double* number. In 64-bit computers, a float can occupy 4 bytes (32 bits) and a double number can occupy 8 bytes (64 bits). Floating numbers are real numbers, as are double numbers. The range of floating numbers is in between $\pm1.18\times10^{-38}$ to $\pm3.4\times10^{38}$, and the double number ranges between $\pm2.23\times10^{-308}$ to $\pm1.80\times10^{308}$. So, you can easily imagine how large a number they can hold in their memory. On an Arduino Uno, both float and double occupy 4 bytes (32 bits) of memory. We will use a float type throughout the entire book when necessary.

Say we have two floating numbers and three double numbers, and the variable names for floats are *myCGPA* and *bookPrice*; for double numbers, the variables are *distance, radius,* and *length.*

So, we can define our floating and double numbers as follows:

```
float myCGPA = 3.89;
float bookPrice = 129.99;
double distance = 53523457.435346;
double radius = 11e+23;
double length = 987902.34532532;
```

Characters and strings

You might remember when you started learning to read. First you learned the alphabet. Then you learned how to construct a word using the alphabet. And finally, you learned how to make long sentences. The same process applies when you need to learn a programming language. You need to know the alphabets (in C, they are called characters; in short, *char),* words, or sentences (we can call this a string, or collection of characters). The character data type can hold only a single symbol or alphabet. Say you need to store a letter (here, *c)* on a variable name, *language.* You need to define the variable as follows:

```
char language = 'c';
```

You cannot assign multiple letters to a character variable. Let's look at an example. You cannot write the following things:

```
char myword = 'Abracadabra';
char testVar = 'Hi, this is me!';
```

If you write the preceding statement to declare your character variable on an IDE, the program will not usually show you an error, but if you look at the output of the variables, you will see only the last character. Let's make it clear. If you want to print the preceding two variables in C, your output will show you only *'a'* and *'!'* for the *myword* and *testVar* variables, respectively. I will explain why you will get these outputs later. So, we can only store a single character on a *char* type variable.

Strings are a collection of characters. A sentence or word can be stored in a string variable. C does not have the data type *String*; people use an array of characters to declare a string in C,but on Arduino Uno, there is *string*. Let's define a *String*:

```
String myText = "This is a lovely day!";
```

On Arduino IDE, you can write the following:

```
Char myText[] = "This is a lovely day!";
```

A character data type in C occupies 1 byte (8 bits) of memory. So, you can easily calculate that, if your word consists of six letters/characters, the string variable would consume 1×6 = 6 bytes of memory; but we must also add an *invisible* byte that indicates the end of the string with a special *null* character, to reach 7 bytes.

Have you noticed that, when we declared our character type variables, we used single quotes, and when we declared our sting type variables we used double quotes? Yes, this is the rule for defining a character and a string. A character need to be inside single quotes and a string needs to be in between double quotes.

Every character has an ASCII number. You can call the character by its ASCII number.

Character A has an ASCII number of 65. We can also print character A by writing the following code:

```
void setup() {
Serial.begin(9600);
Serial.write(65);
}
void loop() {
}
```

Have you noticed we used `Serial.write()` instead of `Serial.print()`? Yes, this is how we print a byte in C for Arduino.

You can test printing other bytes too. Remember, the limit of character bytes is from 33-126 (visible characters). Go to **File | Example | 04. Communication | ASCIITable**. Upload the code to the Arduino Board; you will get full details of all the valid characters in a table.

 ASCII is the short form of **American Standard Code for Information Exchange**. ASCII is used in raw coding and fast coding. We sometimes need to use characters or strings in our programming, but our computer only understands numbers. So, it converts the characters or string into numbers. The ASCII code is the numerical representation of a character. By 65, in ASCII, we mean the character A (capital letter); by 97, we mean character a (lowercase letter).

Booleans

A Boolean is another type of data type in C for Arduino. It represents if something is *true* or *false*. In Arduino IDE, we declare a Boolean data type as follows:

```
boolean testVar;
```

Or:

```
bool testVar;
```

The values of the data type can be assigned as 0 or 1 and true or false (watch the case: False/True instead of false/true will not work). The output of the code will always be 0 or 1. The following shows a full list of how to declare a Boolean variable:

```
bool testbool1 = 0;
bool testbool2 = 1;
bool testbool3 = true;
bool testbool4 = false;
boolean mybool1 = 0;
boolean mybool2 = 1;
boolean mybool3 = true;
boolean mybool4 = false;
```

Let's look at an example. This is not a perfect example. We will look at more usages of Boolean data types in the next chapter.

The following code will print the binary numbers (0 or 1):

```
bool testbool1 = 0;
bool testbool2 = 1;
bool testbool3 = true;
bool testbool4 = false;
boolean mybool1 = 0;
boolean mybool2 = 1;
boolean mybool3 = true;
boolean mybool4 = false;
void setup() {
  Serial.begin(9600);
  Serial.println(testbool1);
  Serial.println(testbool2);
  Serial.println(testbool3);
  Serial.println(testbool4);
  Serial.println(mybool1);
  Serial.println(mybool2);
  Serial.println(mybool3);
  Serial.println(mybool4);
```

```
}
void loop() {

}
```

The output of the code will look like the following screenshot:

See, only binary numbers are printed (no *true* or *false*).

There are other data types in C for Arduino, too. Some of them are byte, array, word, void, and so on. We will use them if we really have to. When we use them, we will also give some descriptions for them. First, we need to know the basic variables and their usages.

Let's learn about all the data types using Arduino IDE.

Collecting and showing data through serial port

Before going any further, let's discuss how we can print something using Arduino IDE. We already printed *Hello Arduino* in the previous chapter. If you don't know how to print something using serial monitor, please go to the previous chapter and then come back here.

Let's recap the print program we used.

We took two functions, setup() and loop(). Inside the setup function, we declared our baud rate as follows:

```
Serial.begin(9600); //default baud for serial communication
```

Right after the baud was defined, we added a special function to print our text on the serial monitor. The function was Serial.print(). Inside the print() function, we wrote (in C we call it *passed*) what we wanted to be seen on the serial monitor.

So, the full code for printing *Hello Arduino* is as follows:

```
void setup(){
  Serial.begin(9600);
  Serial.print("Hello Arduino");
}

void loop() {

}
```

You may know the difference between `Serial.print()` and `Serial.println()`. `Serial.print()` prints a text on **Serial Monitor** without a new line after the text, but `Serial.println()` adds a new line after the text is printed. The following screenshot will help you understand the difference between the two functions:

In the preceding screenshot, you can see I printed three `Serial.print()` functions, one after another, but on the serial monitor, they printed on a single line. I also printed three `Serial.println()` functions, and they were printed as we wanted. We can also use '\n' at the end of our text on the `Serial.print()` function, which will do the same thing as the `Serial.println()` function. From the previous chapter, we know that \n is called an escape sequence.

Let's define a few integer variables and print them on serial monitor. Look at the following code, where we assigned two integer variables, `myNumber01` and `myNumber02`, and printed them using the `Serial.println()` function:

```
    int myNumber01 = 1200;
  void setup() {
    int myNumber02 = 1300;
    Serial.begin(9600);
    Serial.println(myNumber01);
    Serial.println(myNumber02);
  }

  void loop() {

  }
```

Have you noticed I declared the variables in two places? One is declared before the `setup()` function, and another inside the `setup()` function. Amazingly, both are working. Ok, let's make it clear. The `myNumber01` variable is called a **global variable** because it is not inside a function. If any variable is inside a function, it is called a local variable and it is available only in that function. So, `myNumber02` is a local variable, as it is inside the `setup()` function. Let's look at the output of the preceding code:

If we do not want to print a text directly from the `print` function, we do not use quotes inside the `print` function. So, the following code will give you different outputs:

```
int myNumber01 = 1200;
void setup() {
int myNumber02 = 1300;
Serial.begin(9600);
Serial.println(myNumber01);
Serial.println("myNumber02"); //Just added quotations
}
void loop() {
}
```

The output of the code will look like the following screenshot:

Let's print a float and a double number. The code is as follows:

```
    double pie = 3.14159;
    float CGPA = 3.9;
void setup() {
    Serial.begin(9600);
```

```
    Serial.println(pie);
    Serial.println(CGPA);
  }
  void loop() {
  }
```

The output will be similar to the following screenshot:

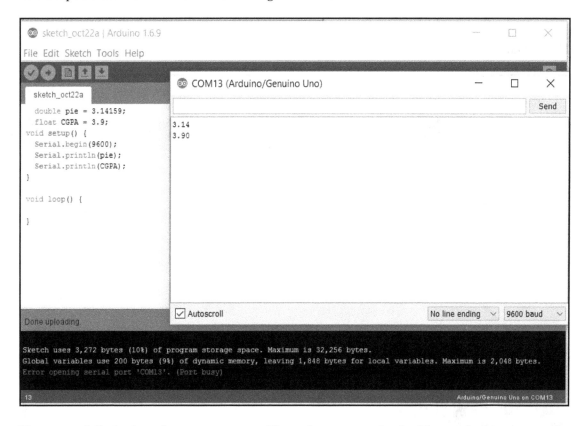

If you carefully look at the output, you will see the output of a double number is not exactly what we wrote. On Arduino Uno, float and double numbers are basically the same while printed via the `print()` function. The `print()` function prints only two decimal digits by default. Both float and double can hold the input of two digits after the decimal. Since both have a limit to hold a number, let's assign some long number to a double variable and see what happens. Perhaps your Arduino gets blasted. Just kidding. Let's look at what happens on our output. The code is as follows:

```
double longNumber= 847982635862956295.982378295327;
double negativeLongNumber = -947973249864967657.9304709372409832;
```

```
void setup() {
  Serial.begin(9600);
  Serial.println(longNumber);
  Serial.println(negativeLongNumber);
}

void loop() {

}
```

The output will be similar to the following screenshot:

By **ovf,** we mean overflow. This means the number we assigned to our variables is larger than the limit of the data type.

The same thing happens with the integer data type. Can you check it at home? Don't worry, your Arduino won't burn.

Let's take the input of some data types.

If we want to take input from a keyboard, we need to check if there is available data incoming from the serial monitor. To check this, we need to use a condition. For now, let's remember to include the following line after your baud rate (it can be inside the `loop()` function too, if you want to repeatedly check the serial and want to send data):

```
while (Serial.available() == 0);
```

Now, let's declare a global variable. In my case, it is as follows:

```
int letmego;
```

After the code, while `(Serial.available() == 0);`, write the following code:

```
letmego = Serial.parseInt();
```

The `Serial.parseInt()` function will convert the received byte from the serial monitor into an integer and store it to our variable. Then we just need to print the variable. Look at the full code for a clear idea:

```
int letmego;
void setup() {
  Serial.begin(9600);
  while (Serial.available() == 0);
  letmego = Serial.parseInt();
  Serial.print("Your input is: ");
  Serial.println(letmego);
}
void loop() {

}
```

The output of the preceding code will be similar to the following screenshot, where I input on serial monitor 255:

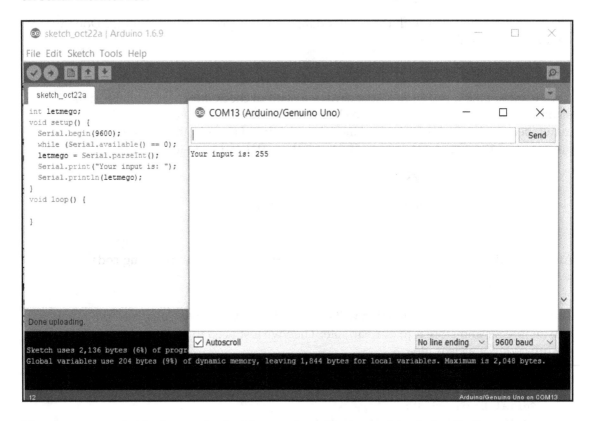

If you want to take the input of a double number, all you need to change is the `Serial.parseInt()` function, to `Serial.parseFloat()`. Look at the following code, with output, where the input was 123.57:

```
float letmego;
void setup() {
  Serial.begin(9600);
  while (Serial.available() == 0);
  letmego = Serial.parseFloat();
  Serial.print("Your input is: ");
  Serial.println(letmego);
}
void loop() {

}
```

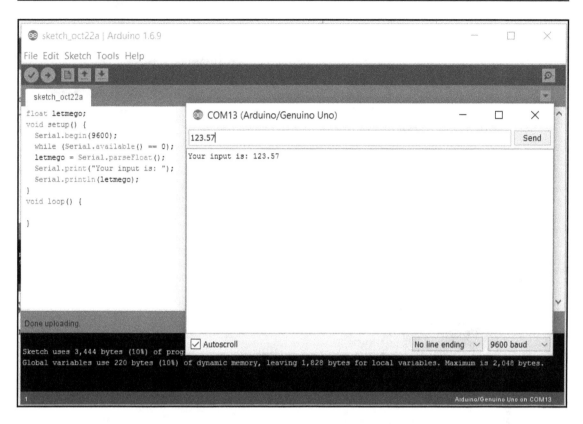

If you want to read a character using the serial monitor, you need change the
`Serial.parseFloat()` function into `Serial.read()` and set our variable as a character.
Look at the following program, with output, where the input from the serial monitor was *A*:

```
char letmego; //data type changed
void setup() {
  Serial.begin(9600);
  while (Serial.available() == 0);
  letmego = Serial.read(); //function changed
  Serial.print("Your input is: ");
  Serial.println(letmego);
}
void loop() {
}
```

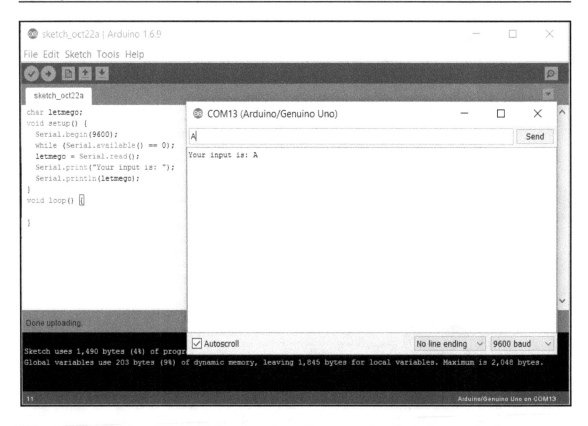

If you want to take an input of full string, then all you need to do is change the data type into String and change the Serial.read() function to Serial.readString(). Look at the following example, with output, where the input was *To be or not to be, that is the question*:

```
String letmego;
void setup() {
  Serial.begin(9600);
  while (Serial.available() == 0);
  letmego = Serial.readString();
  Serial.print("Your input is: ");
  Serial.println(letmego);
}
void loop() {

}
```

Mathematical operations

Let x = 89, y = 98 and z = 45. What is the sum of three variables? You can sum up the values of x, y, and z and tell me the number. But since we have been learning C for Arduino, let's go a little further. We can do these kinds of mathematical operations using Arduino IDE – not just the easy mathematical operations, but far more complex mathematics can be solved using C for Arduino IDE.

Before going any further, let's learn about some arithmetic symbols used in Arduino programming. They are also called arithmetic operators:

+	**Addition**
–	Subtraction
*	Multiplication
/	Division
%	Modulus

Addition

By definition, addition sums two or more numbers. In C for Arduino, addition will do the same. This operation will add two or more numbers and store them in a variable. Let's look at an example.

We started the *Mathematical operations* section with a question to sum up three variables (x = 89, y = 98, and z = 45). Let's find the sum using Arduino programming.

We have three numbers. All numbers here are integers. We can assign them to be integer variables as follows:

```
int x = 89;
int y = 98;
int z = 45;
```

Now store them in another integer variable, say, the variable is `sum`:

```
int sum;
```

Store the sum of the variables (x, y, and z) into the variable *sum*, as follows:

```
sum = x+ y+ z;
```

 The addition/subtraction/division/multiplication will be integers or double, if the operands are integers or double, respectively. Say, if the operands are integers, the output after the mathematical operation will also be integers. If they were double, the output will also be double.

Now print the variable *sum* on the serial monitor:

```
Serial.print(sum);
```

The full code and output will be as follows:

```
int x = 89;
int y = 98;
int z = 45;
int sum;

void setup() {
Serial.begin(9600);
sum = x=y+z;
Serial.print("The sum of x, y and z is: "); // This line was written
without any purpose. Just to fancy the output.
Serial.print(sum);
}
void loop() {

}
```

Now if you had 10 variables to sum up, I'm sure you could find the sum of them. Consider a problem: You have 23 pens, 25 pencils, 56 books, 32 apples, 89 oranges, 45 erasers, 87 bananas, and 98 chocolates. Make a list of two categories – food and non-food – and print the total number of food and non-food items using arithmetic operations.

The preceding problem has four foods (apples, oranges, bananas, and chocolates). So, we will sum them up and store them in a variable called `food`. For non-foods, we have pens, pencils, books, and erasers. We will store the sum inside another variable, called `non_food`.

So, our variables should be declared as follows:

```
int pens = 23;
int pencils = 25;
int books = 56;
int apples =32;
int oranges = 89;
int erasers = 45;
int bananas = 87;
int chocolates = 98;
int food;
int non_food;
```

Now, let's assign the `food` and *non_food* variables with proper item values:

```
food = apples + oranges + bananas + chocolates;
non_food = pens + pencils + books + erasers;
```

Finally, we will print both the variables. The full code of the program and output is as follows:

```
int pens = 23;
int pencils = 25;
int books = 56;
int apples = 32;
int oranges = 89;
int erasers = 45;
int bananas = 87;
int chocolates = 98;
int food;
int non_food;

void setup() {
  Serial.begin(9600);
  food = apples + oranges + bananas + chocolates;
  non_food = pens + pencils + books + erasers;

  Serial.print("You have ");
```

```
  Serial.print(food);
  Serial.println(" food items");
  Serial.print("You have ");
  Serial.print(non_food);
  Serial.print(" non food items");
}
void loop() {

}
```

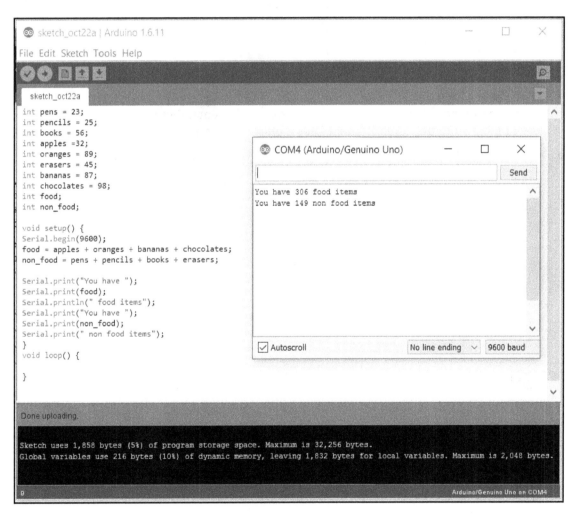

You can declare a variable in one, also; say you need to declare three double variables (num1, num2, and num3). You can declare these as follows:

```
double num1, num2, num3;
```

This is similar to the following declaration:

double num1; double num2; double num3; You can also declare any type of data type on a single line. If your variables have something assigned to them, you can write them as follows (where all are float and have the values num1 = 3.7, num2 = 87.9, and num3 = 8.9): float num1 = 3.7, num2 = 87.9, num3 = 8.9;

Subtraction

We can subtract a number from another number. By subtraction, we mean the difference between two numbers. From your math class, you might remember that we subtract the smaller number from the large number. Let's look at an example.

Say you have 649 red LEDs (Light Emitting Diodes) and 756 blue LEDs. You have used 123 red LEDs and 87 blue LEDs on a project. How many LEDs do you have now?

Let's declare our variables first:

```
int initialRedLED = 649, initialBlueLED = 756, spentRedLED = 123,
spentBlueLED = 87, finalTotalLEDs, finalRedLED, finalBlueLED;
// We have declared all our variables in one line.
```

We now find the difference between initial and spent LEDs, and store them in another two variables (finalRedLED and finalBlueLED) as follows:

```
finalRedLED = initialRedLED - spentRedLED; //to find the difference
finalBlueLED = initialBlueLED - spentBlueLED; //to find the difference
```

Now print our variables finalRedLED and finalBlueLED.

To get the total LEDs left, we need to add the finalRedLED and finalBlueLED, and store them on another variable, finalTotalLEDs, and print finalTotalLEDs. So, our final code and output will be as follows:

```
int initialRedLED = 649, initialBlueLED = 756, spentRedLED = 123,
spentBlueLED = 87, finalTotalLEDs, finalRedLED, finalBlueLED;
void setup() {
  Serial.begin(9600);
  finalRedLED = initialRedLED - spentRedLED;
  finalBlueLED = initialBlueLED - spentBlueLED;
  finalTotalLEDs = finalRedLED + finalBlueLED;
```

```
    Serial.print("Initial Blue LEDs = ");
    Serial.println(initialBlueLED);
    Serial.print("Initial Red LEDs = ");
    Serial.println(initialRedLED);
    Serial.print("Final Red LEDs = ");
    Serial.println(finalRedLED);
    Serial.print("Finalt Blue LEDS = ");
    Serial.println(finalBlueLED);
    Serial.print("Total LEDs finally = ");
    Serial.print(finalTotalLEDs);

}
void loop() {

}
```

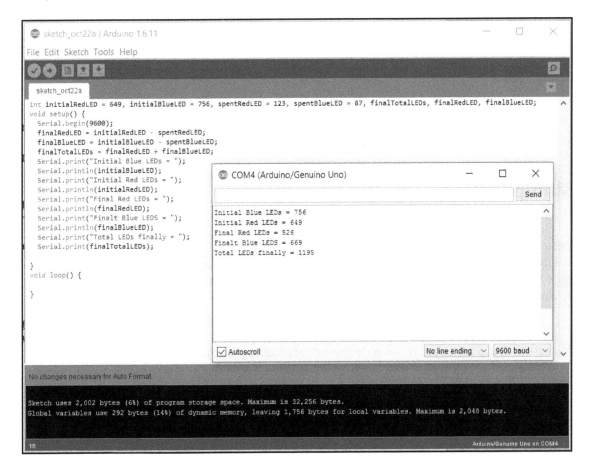

Exercise

1. Find the difference between 3.0×10^8 and 2.9×10^8 (hint: double x = 3.0E8 and double y = 2.9E8).
2. Find the difference between 23 January 1960 and 4 July 2020 (hint: take three variables for day, month, and year for the first date, and for the second date, do the same. Use a numerical format for the month, that is, January is 1, February is 2, March is 3, and so on).
3. Can you write the output of the following code?

```
void setup() {
  Serial.begin(9600);
  Serial.write(65);
  Serial.write(114);
  Serial.write(100);
  Serial.write(117);
  Serial.write(105);
  Serial.write(110);
  Serial.write(111);
  Serial.write(33);
}
void loop() {
}
```

Multiplication

If you want to multiply a number with another number, you can do it using C for Arduino.

Let's consider another scenario. Suppose you have four books. Each book has 850 pages on average. You want to find the total number of pages of the book. You can simply add 850 four times, or you can multiply 850 by 4. That will be the number of pages. In C for Arduino, we will first declare a few variables, as follows:

```
int numberOfBooks = 4, numberOfPages = 850, totalPageNumbers;
```

Inside out setup function, we will do the calculations as follows:

```
totalPageNumbers = numberOfBooks * numberOfPages;
```

Then we will print the variable, `totalPagenumbers`. The full code, with output, will be as follows:

```
int numberOfBooks = 4, numberOfPages = 850, totalPageNumbers;
void setup() {
```

```
Serial.begin(9600);
totalPageNumbers = numberOfBooks * numberOfPages;
Serial.print("Total books numbers ");
Serial.println(numberOfBooks);
Serial.print("Page numbers per book ");
Serial.println(numberOfPages);
Serial.print("Total numbers of pages ");
Serial.println(totalPageNumbers);
}
void loop() {
}
```

Let's write a program that can find the total number of pages of a number of books, input by the user.

Say we will input the number of books, and pages of each book. Our program will print the total number of pages.

From the input section of this chapter, you already know how you can take input of an integer. Now we will do another thing, to take integers, store inside a variable, and use them for calculations.

Declare three variables as follows:

```
int numberOfBooks, numberOfPages, totalPageNumber;
```

Take input of the number of book by the following line:

```
numberOfBooks = Serial.parseInt();
```

Before that, use a `delay()` function with a time parameter. The Arduino board will wait that much time for the input on the serial monitor. Then take another variable input the same as the previous one. The code will be as follows:

```
int numberOfBooks, numberOfPages, totalPageNumber;
void setup() {
Serial.begin(9600);
Serial.print("Input Number of books\n");
delay(1000); // Arduino will wait 1 sec for the input
numberOfBooks = Serial.parseInt();
Serial.print("Input Number of pages\n");
delay(1000); // Arduino will wait 1 sec for the input
numberOfPages = Serial.parseInt();
totalPageNumber = numberOfBooks * numberOfPages;
Serial.print("Total Number of pages\n");
Serial.print(totalPageNumber);
}
void loop() {
}
```

Let's look at the output with an input of 30 (number of books) and 560 (number of pages per book) The output will look as follows:

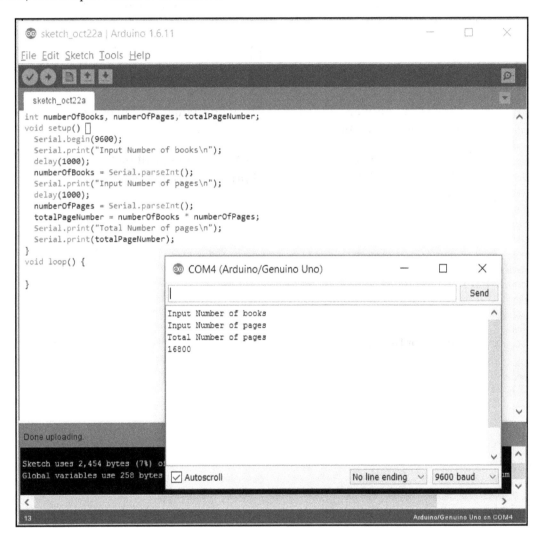

You can practise the following exercise at home:

1. Take input of three float variables (u, t, and a) and find the distance (s) from the following equation:

$$S = ut + \frac{1}{2}at^2$$

   (Hints: t^2 is equivalent to t*t in C. The whole equation will be s = u*t+0.5*a*t*t. To take input of a float, use *Serial.parseFloat ()*)

2. Take inputs of three numbers and one character, and print them onto one line.
3. Take input of two double numbers and print them onto two lines.
4. Take input of an asterisk (*) and print as follows:

```
a.  *
**
***
b.  ***
**
*
c.  *  **  ***
```

5. Take input of two characters (*V* and *A*) and two integers (*0* and *1*), and print them as follows:

```
a.  VA01
b.  01AV
c.  0AV1
d.  000V
e.  VVVV
f.  VAVAVA
```

Division

We can divide a number with another, but we need to know the basic rules of division in C.

Say we will divide 30 with 5. Since both are integers and 30 is totally divisible by 5, there will be no problem with the output. But if we wanted to divide 30 with 7, we will get 4.28 if we declare all the variables as float. If we declare our variables as integers, then our result will be 4. Look at the examples in the following screenshots.

If we declare our variables as integers and the first number is totally divisible by the second number, the output will be as follows:

If we declare our variables as integers and the first number is not totally divisible by the second number, the output will be as follows:

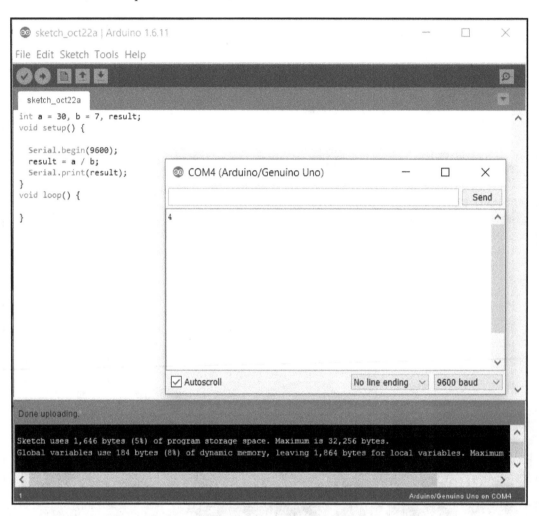

If we declare our variables as floats and the first number is totally divisible by the second number, the output will be as follows:

If we declare our variables as floats and the first number is not totally divisible by the second number, the output will be as follows:

So, we will have to be careful in finding the result of a division. We will follow the last method, where we used all the variables to be floats to avoid any wrong answers.

Let's look at an example.

Suppose your electronics shop has 100 Arduinos that cost a total of $500 and you sold 20 Arduinos ($6.75 per Arduino). Find out the profit.

Now, define our variables:

```
float initialArduinos = 100.0, initialTotalPrice = 500.0, numberOfSell =
20.0, sellingPrice = 6.75, costPrice, totalSellingPrice, totalCostPrice,
totalProfit;
```

Now it's time for some simple mathematics:

```
  costPrice = initialTotalPrice / initialArduinos; // found per Arduino
price
  Serial.print("Each arduino cost $");
  Serial.println(costPrice);
  totalCostPrice = costPrice * numberOfSell; // found total cost price
  Serial.print("Total cost price for 20 Arduinos  $");
  Serial.println(totalCostPrice);
  totalSellingPrice = numberOfSell * sellingPrice ; // found total selling
price
  Serial.print("Total selling price for 20 Arduinos  $");
  Serial.println(totalSellingPrice);
  totalProfit = totalSellingPrice - totalCostPrice;  // found the profit
for 20 arduinos.
  Serial.print("The total profil is $");
  Serial.println(totalProfit);
```

The output of the code will be as follows:

Modulus

The *modulus* operator finds out the remainder. Say you want to divide 25 by 4. What will your remainder be? 4×6 =24. So, if we divide 25 by 4, we will get the result 4, and the remainder will be 1.

In C for Arduino, a modulus operator is the % symbol. The representation of 25 *modulus* 4 is 25%4, which is equal to 1. So, we can write 25%4 = 1.

Let's look at an example:

Find out the remainders if 623 is divided by 4, 5, 6, 7, 8, and 9.

Let's declare our variables.

```
int myNumber = 623, remainder;
```

Now find the remainder:

```
Remainder = myNumber % 4; // or 5/6/7/8/9
```

Now print the remainder. So, the total code, with output, will look as follows:

```
int myNumber = 623, reminder;
void setup() {
  Serial.begin(9600);
  reminder = myNumber % 4;
  Serial.print("reminder by 4 is ");
  Serial.println(reminder);

  reminder = myNumber % 5;
  Serial.print("reminder by 5 is ");
  Serial.println(reminder);

  reminder = myNumber % 6;
  Serial.print("reminder by 6 is ");
  Serial.println(reminder);

  reminder = myNumber % 7;
  Serial.print("reminder by 7 is ");
  Serial.println(reminder);

  reminder = myNumber % 8;
  Serial.print("reminder by 8 is ");
  Serial.println(reminder);

  reminder = myNumber % 9;
  Serial.print("reminder by 9 is ");
  Serial.println(reminder);
}
void loop() {

}
```

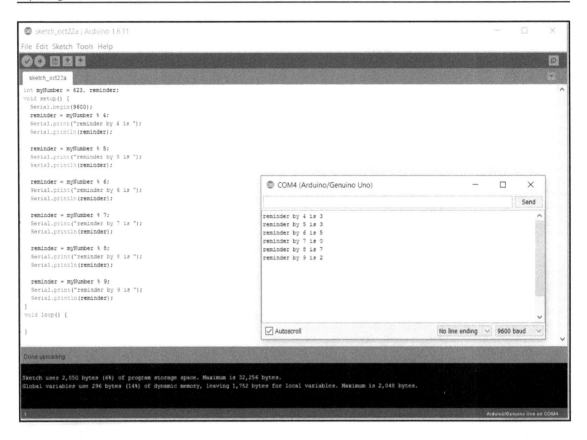

There are more mathematical operations. We will learn about them as needed, in the following chapters.

Arrays

C for Arduino provides users the capability to design a set of the same data type. This functionality is called an **array.** An array is a collection of the same data type into one variable.

Let's consider the following code:

```
int x;
void setup() {
    x = 23;
    x = 78;
    Serial.begin(9600);
    Serial.print(x);
```

```
}
void loop() {

}
```

Can you tell me the output of this code?

x was defined as an integer as a global variable. Later, inside the `setup()` function, it was first assigned to number 23, and second to 78. No doubt the output will be 78, because it was defined later and C reads the program line by line, or from top to bottom. To avoid the complexity, we use arrays.

Say we need to store 100 same-type variables and use them later. We can do this in two ways:

- Take 100 variables and assign values to them
- Take a single variable and store all values to it

The second option is easy and less time consuming. Now, the burning question is, how can we declare an array? Well, it's simple. Let's look at an example first:

```
int myArray[5] = {3,5,7,8,3};
```

Look at the following screenshot:

```
How many number will an Array contain
                    ⇩
myArray[5]= {3,5,7,8,3};
        Index number: 0  1  2  3  4
```

myArray is the name of the variable, and inside the brackets, there is 5, which is the limit of the array. This means how many variables the array can contain. This number fits your need; you can declare any number you want. On the right-hand side, there are five numbers (as our array can contain five variables) inside curly brackets, separated by commas. Each number has an index number by which we will call our variables. The index numbers start from 0. So, our first number (which is 3) can be called by `myArray[0]`. If we print `myArray[0]`, we will get 3. Similarly, if we call `myArray[1]`, we will get 5, and so on. Let's check it with the following code:

```
int myArray[5] = {3, 5, 7, 8, 3};
```

```
void setup() {

  Serial.begin(9600);
  Serial.print("Index number is 0 and the value is ");
  Serial.println(myArray[0]);
  Serial.print("Index number is 1 and the value is ");
  Serial.println(myArray[1]);
  Serial.print("Index number is 2 and the value is ");
  Serial.println(myArray[2]);
  Serial.print("Index number is 3 and the value is ");
  Serial.println(myArray[3]);
  Serial.print("Index number is 4 and the value is ");
  Serial.println(myArray[4]);
}
void loop() {

}
```

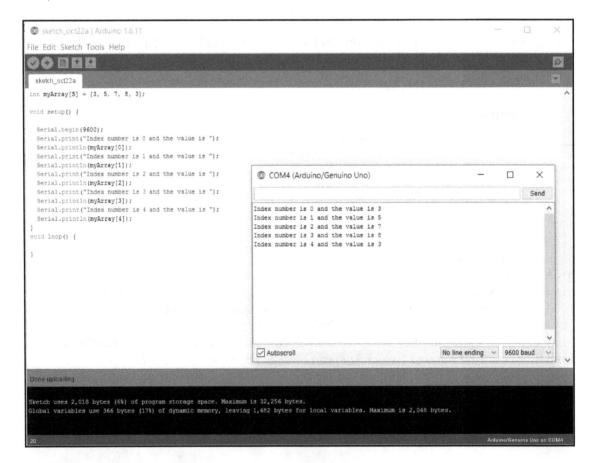

The final index number is N-1, where n is the number inside brackets []. So, we cannot call the index number N or greater than N. We cannot even call a negative index number . What would happen if we called them? Let's look at the following code and output:

```cpp
int myArray[5] = {3, 5, 7, 8, 3};

void setup() {

  Serial.begin(9600);
  Serial.print("Index number is -1 and the value is ");
  Serial.println(myArray[-1]); //negative index number
  Serial.print("Index number is 5 and the value is ");
  Serial.println(myArray[5]); // N index number
  Serial.print("Index number is 6 and the value is ");
  Serial.println(myArray[6]); // Greater than N index number.
}
void loop() {

}
```

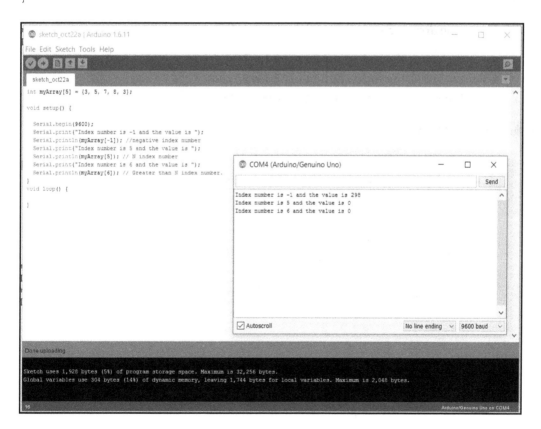

From the output, you can see that, when we called an index which is less than N, we get a number. For now, we call it a garbage number. It is not in our array. This is because the microcontroller reserves its memory for the data types. If we call the memory location, we get something stored in the location. If nothing is there, we get zero. That is why, when we called the index equal to N, we got 0. There is nothing in the memory. The same thing happened when we called the index greater than N.

The data type of an array can be anything (integers, double, float, character, bytes, Boolean, and so on). Let's look at another example.

Suppose a class has 20 students. You took an exam worth 50 marks and you need to store all the marks in your program according to roll numbers. We know that it is not wise to make 20 variables and call them one by one when necessary, as long as we can use an array. So, let's use an array and find the numbers of roll number 3, 7, and 16. First, declare our variable. The marks cannot be integers, so we take our variable as float:

```
float marks[20] = {45.5, 23.2, 0, 34, 45.9, 50, 12, 33, 34.5,0, 23.9, 15,
18, 17.4, 18.3, 10, 4, 9, 34.8, 4.5};
```

Now, we print the array according to our index number.

- For the roll 3, the index number is 3-1 = 2.
- For the roll 7, the index number is 7-1 = 6.
- For the roll 16, the index number is 16-1 = 15.

The full code will be as follows:

```
float marks[20] = {45.5, 23.2, 0, 34, 45.9, 50, 12, 33, 34.5, 0, 23.9, 15,
18, 17.4, 18.3, 10, 4, 9, 34.8, 4.5};

void setup() {

  Serial.begin(9600);
  Serial.print("Mark obtained by roll 3 is  ");
  Serial.println(marks[2]); //roll number 3's marks
  Serial.print("Mark obtained by roll 7 is  ");
  Serial.println(marks[6]); //roll number 7's marks
  Serial.print("Mark obtained by roll 16 is  ");
  Serial.println(marks[15]); //roll number 16's marks

}
void loop() {

}
```

The output of the code will be as follows:

Let's do the same thing with two arrays containing the roll numbers of the students. This time, we will print the marks obtained by the students and their roll numbers for roll 1, 4, 8, 7, and 9.

Our second array will be defined as follows:

```
int roll [20] = {1,2,3,4,5,6,7,8,9,10,11,12,13,14,15,16,17,18,19,20};
```

Now we will print the roll numbers and marks according to the following code:

```
float marks[20] = {45.5, 23.2, 0, 34, 45.9, 50, 12, 33, 34.5, 0, 23.9, 15,
18, 17.4, 18.3, 10, 4, 9, 34.8, 4.5};
int roll [20] = {1, 2, 3, 4, 5, 6, 7, 8, 9, 10, 11, 12, 13, 14, 15, 16, 17,
18, 19, 20};
void setup() {

  Serial.begin(9600);
  Serial.print("Mark obtained by roll ");
  Serial.print(roll[0]); //this is roll number 1, since the first element
of the array.
  Serial.print(": ");
  Serial.println(marks[0]); //roll number 1's marks
  Serial.print("Mark obtained by roll ");
  Serial.print(roll[3]); //this is roll number 4, since the first element
of the array.
  Serial.print(": ");
  Serial.println(marks[3]); //roll number 4's marks
  Serial.print("Mark obtained by roll ");
  Serial.print(roll[7]); //this is roll number 8, since the first element
of the array.
  Serial.print(": ");
  Serial.println(marks[7]); //roll number 1's marks
  Serial.print("Mark obtained by roll ");
  Serial.print(roll[6]); //this is roll number 7, since the first element
of the array.
  Serial.print(": ");
  Serial.println(marks[6]); //roll number 1's marks
  Serial.print("Mark obtained by roll ");
  Serial.print(roll[8]); //this is roll number 9, since the first element
of the array.
  Serial.print(": ");
  Serial.println(marks[8]); //roll number 9's marks
}
void loop() {

}
```

Let's check the output:

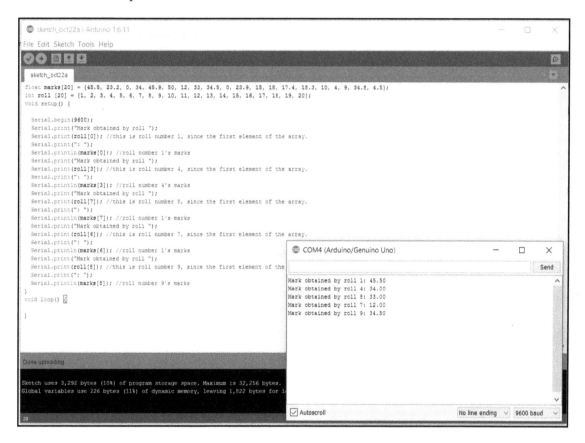

Look at the index numbers we used. I hope you understand the meaning of index number now.

If you want to make an array of characters (a, e, i, o, and u), your array will look as follows:

```
char vowel[5] = {'a', 'e', 'i', 'o', 'u'};
```

If you call by the third index, you will get o, since by the third index, we mean the fourth position of the array list. Let's look at the output:

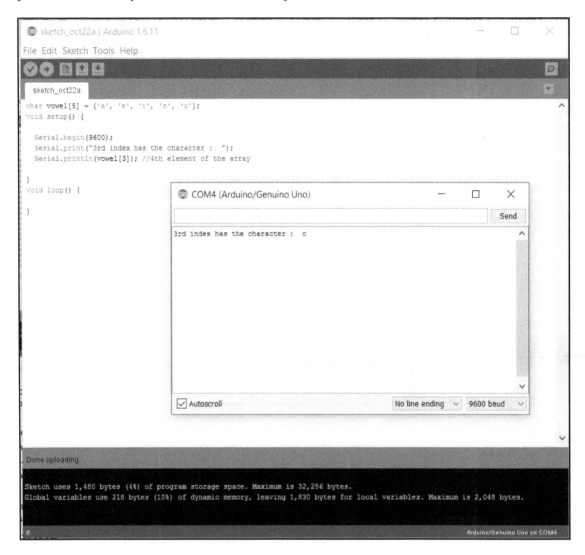

Each character should have single quotes, as we declared before. We will discuss how you can declare String arrays later.

Finally, we can say that an array is a collection of similar elements. The similar elements can be all integers, floats, doubles, characters, bytes, and so on.

We have learned about single-dimensional arrays. There are also multi-dimensional arrays. Let's look at an example.

You may have heard of a matrix in your math class. In the following code, A, B, and C are three matrices:

$$A = \begin{matrix} 1 & 4 & 6 \\ 8 & 9 & 11 \\ 23 & 4 & 5 \end{matrix} \quad B = \begin{matrix} 2 & 5 \\ 6 & 7 \end{matrix} \text{ and } C = \begin{matrix} 2 & 5 & 7 \\ 10 & 4 & 6 \end{matrix}$$

- The number of rows and columns of matrix A is 3×3 (read 3 by 3)
- The number of rows and columns of matrix B is 2×2 (read 2 by 2)
- The number of rows and columns of matrix C is 2×3 (read 2 by 3)

So, the total elements can be found by multiplying the rows and columns. The convention is writing the numbers of the rows first, followed by the numbers of the columns, when we write the dimensions of a matrix (that is, rows × columns) The B matrix in C for Arduino can be written as follows:

```
int B[2][2] ={{2,5},{6,7}};
```

If we want to call the first element of the first row, we can call it by printing the following array with 0 and 0 indexes:

```
Serial.print(B[0][0]);
```

The second element of the first row is as follows:

```
Serial.print(B[0][1]);
```

The first element of the second array is as follows:

```
Serial.print(B[1][0]);
```

The second element of the second row is as follows:

```
Serial.print(B[1][1]);
```

Let's call the whole matrix in a program; the code will be as follows:

```
int B[2][2] = {{2, 5}, {5, 7}};
void setup() {
  Serial.begin(9600);
  Serial.print(B[0][0]);
  Serial.print(" ");
  Serial.println(B[0][1]);
```

```
    Serial.print(B[1][0]);
    Serial.print(" ");
    Serial.print(B[1][1]);


  }
  void loop() {

  }
```

The output of the code will be as follows:

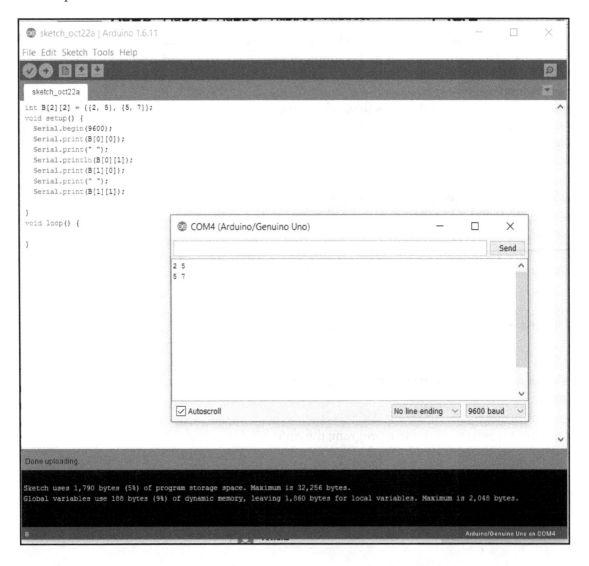

Exercise

1. Make a list of the following food items, with the prices next to them. If a customer buys five pieces of food item c. on the list and five pieces of food item e. on the list, calculate the total money he would need to buy the food items:
   1. Sandwiches ($2.90)
   2. Burgers ($4.90)
   3. Pizzas ($9.99)
   4. Soft Drinks ($1.50)
   5. Beer ($4.99)

   Your output should look as follows:

```
****The customer receipt****
Food Name Quantity Price Total
Sandwiches 0 2.90 0
Burgers 0 4.90 0
Pizzas 5 9.99 49.95
Soft Drinks 0 1.50 0
Beer 5 4.99 24.95
Total: $ 74.90
```

   (Hints: Make two array lists for the quantity and price of each items. Then multiply the array with the correct index number. You will find the total prices. Then, sum up all the prices.)

2. Assume you have the following array:

```
char symbol [10] = {'!', '@', '#', '$', '%', '&', '*', '+', '=', '_'};
```

   Now write the following programs for the following outputs:@

```
@ #@#
$@#@$@#@
&$@#@$@#@
!!!!!!!!!!*!!!!!!!!!!
%%%%****%%%%
*^E^&!$#@(
```

3. Write a program for the following output using modulus, arrays, and other mathematical operators:

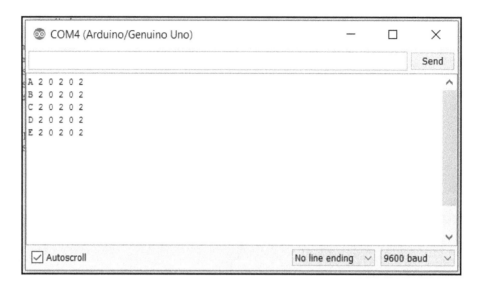

(Hints: Take two arrays. One is five characters and another is five integers. Then find the modulus of the number arrays by 4. Finally, print them.)

Print the sum of the following matrices:

$$A = \begin{matrix} 9 & 3 \\ 8 & 7 \\ 6 & 0 \end{matrix} \quad \text{and} \quad B = \begin{matrix} 6 & 8 \\ 5 & 5 \\ 1 & 2 \end{matrix}$$

If we used *loops* for our program, the program would have been much easier. We will learn about *loops* in the next chapter (Blinking with Operations and Loops).

Strings and operations with strings

A string is one of the most important data types in C for Arduino. In this section, we will learn more about string.

By string, we mean a collection of characters. A sentence or word is a string.

In pure C, we don't have the data type `String`, but in C for Arduino, we do. Let's look at a basic program using the string data type:

```
String myString = "Hello, How are you?";
void setup() {
  Serial.begin(9600);
  Serial.print(myString);
}
void loop() {

}
```

The output of the program is as follows:

The output is a plain text that we assigned to our `String` variable, *myString*. If your string is too long, you can write it as follows:

```
String myString = " This is the first line"
                  " This is the second line"
                  " This is the third line"
                  " This is the fourth line"
                  " This is the fifth line";
void setup() {
  Serial.begin(9600);
  Serial.print(myString);

}
void loop() {

}
```

The output of the preceding code will be as follows:

Have you noticed that all our output is on one line? Yes, it will be on one single line, even though the string has multiple lines. If we want to use a break after each line, we need to use an escape character (\n). With the use of \n, the code's output will be as follows:

Conversion of strings

Other kinds of data types can be converted into a `String` data type.

Let's look at few examples.

If you want to convert a character into a `String`, you can do the following:

```
String myString = String('A');
```

To convert an integer into a `String`, you can write the following:

```
String myString = String(55);
```

You can convert a string into a `String` object too (we will learn more about objects in later chapters):

```
String myString = String("This String is an object String");
```

You can convert a decimal number into binary (2-base number: 0 and 1), hexadecimal (16-base number: 0-9 and A-F) or octal (8-base number: 0 to 7), by changing it as follows:

```
String myString = String(44,BIN); // change decimal to binary
String myString = String(44,HEX); //change decimal to hexadecimal
String myString = String(44,OCT); //change decimal to octal
```

If you want to keep a definite decimal point, you can write your float as follows:

```
String myString = String(44.453534,5); //. This will show up to five decimal
```
places.

Let's look at the preceding conversation in one code:

```
String myStringString = String('A');
String myStringInt = String(55);
String myStringObject = String("This is a String Object");
String myStringBin = String(44, BIN);
String myStringHexa = String(44, HEX);
String myStringOcta = String(44, OCT);
String myStringDecimal = String(44.453534, 5);
void setup() {
  Serial.begin(9600);
  Serial.println(myStringString);
  Serial.println(myStringInt);
  Serial.println(myStringObject);
  Serial.println(myStringBin);
  Serial.println(myStringHexa);
  Serial.println(myStringOcta);
```

```
      Serial.println(myStringDecimal);
   }
   void loop() {

   }
```

The output will be as follows:

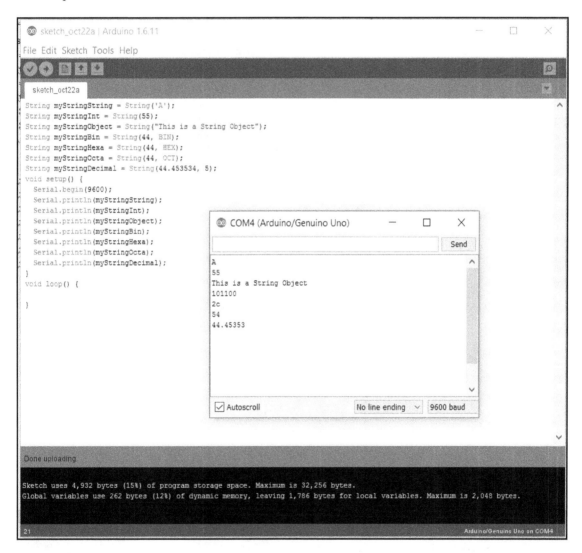

You can add two strings in a few ways. This process is known as concatenation. Let's assume we have two strings, as follows:

```
String A = "Hello, Arduino! ";
String B = "How are you today? ";
```

If we want to join the strings together, we can do the following:

```
String C = A + B;
```

Now, if we print `String C`, we will get the following output:

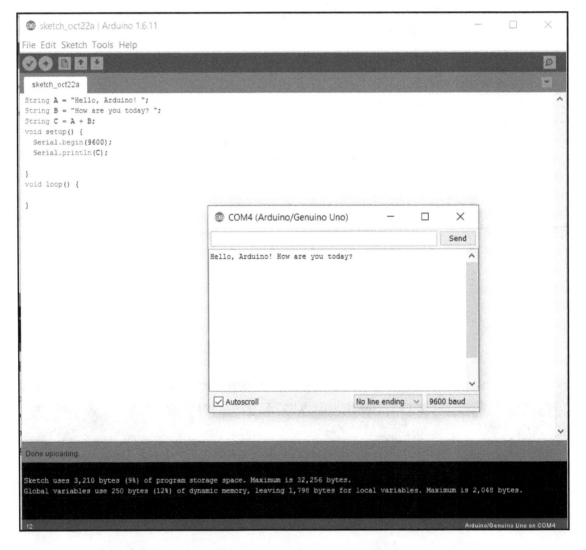

We can also concatenate `Strings` and numbers, as follows:

```
int numb = 90;
String D = "The result is " + numb;
```

The output will look as follows:

You can replace part of a string with another string. We have the following string:

```
String A = "Hello, My name is Arduino!";
```

Now, we want to replace *"Hello"* with *"Hi"*. We can do this as follows:

```
String B = A.replace("Hello", "Hi");
```

Now, the new String B is `"Hi, My name is Arduino!";`.

Let's look at the output:

There are lots of operations using strings. We will learn about more operations in later chapters.

Exercise

1. Write a program that will print the following outputs (using string operations):

   "This is my Lab; it has 2 doors" (use concatenation here and print 2 from another variable).

   Make a list of arrays (two-dimensional) and multiply all the elements by 100.

2. Construct a single-dimensional array of integers, convert all the elements into String, and then add a suffix to them (if an element of your array is 6, make it look like *6arduino*).

3. Build two arrays of integers (any dimension you want). Make the rows and columns the same (if multi-dimensional). Then divide the first array with the second array, and store it into another array. Later, print them. (Hints: Suppose your arrays are $A = 6 \quad 2 \quad 1$ and $B = 1 \quad 2 \quad 2$, the third array should be $C = 6.0 \quad 1.0 \quad 0.5$.)

4. Write a program that will have the following output:

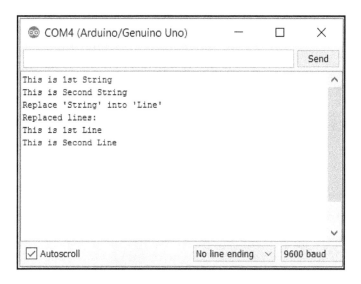

Summary

In this chapter, we have looked at the basic ideas of C programming on Arduino IDE. We learned about variables, data types, arrays, and strings. We have also learned about a few operations using strings. To those who are new to both Arduino programming and C programming, my advice is, don't skip this chapter. Study the whole chapter carefully and do all the exercises assigned to you. Remember, do not copy the code from the book directly; it may cause errors on the Arduino IDE, since Arduino does not support Unicode character encodings.

If you have done all the exercises and studied the chapter, then you are most welcome to move onto the next chapter, Blinking with Operations and Loops, where we will learn about more exciting features of Arduino.

4
Blinking with Operations and Loops

If I say a circle looks like a rectangle, would you oppose my statement? Yes, you would. Why? Because a circle is a round-shaped object, whereas the rectangle has four angles. In your brain, you have images of both circles and rectangles. You just compared a circle to a rectangle and opposed my statement. This is how logic works. We compare with something and decide if our statement is true or false. In this chapter, we are going to learn about logical operations with **Arduino IDE**. We will also learn about loops.

Expression in C

Before we learn about logical operations, let's look at a few expressions in C programming. Suppose you need to identify the larger of two numbers (100 and 200). You will definitely say 200 is larger than 100, right? The question is, how did you get your answer? Yes, by comparing the numbers with each other. The condition is 100<200, or 200>100. The two symbols (< and >) are known as *less than* and *greater than*. Let's look at a few more expressions:

Expression	Meaning
x == y	x is equal to y.
x != y	x is not equal to y.
x < y	x is less than y.
x > y	x is greater than y.
x <= y	x is less than or equal to y.

x >= y	x is greater than or equal to y.

Remember, we use double equal signs (==), not a single equal sign (=) to indicate a data type is equal to another. The preceding expressions only work when we use logical conditions in C.

Logical operations in C

Sometimes, an event may depend on something. Say, if the weather is good, I will go outside. If I can connect my Arduino to my PC properly, I will be able to code for it. If it is Sunday, I will be sleeping the whole day, and so on. All these sentences depend on certain conditions. If something happens, then something will be done.

If-statement

Look at the following figure for a clear idea:

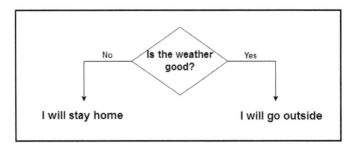

The figure shows you two options: *Yes* and *No*. If the weather is good (**Yes**), then I will go outside, and if the weather is bad (**No**), I won't go outside. Remember, the main logic here is, if an something occurs, something else will be done or not done. In Arduino for C, we call this logical operation an *if-condition*.

Let's look at an example on our Arduino IDE.

Fire up your Arduino IDE and write the following code first. I will explain the code a little bit later:

```
String condition;
void setup() {
  Serial.begin(9600);
  condition = "No"; // set condition's value
  if (condition == "Yes") {
    Serial.println("I will go outside");
  }
  if (condition == "No") {
    Serial.println("I will not go outside");
  }
}
void loop() {

}
```

Can you guess the output from the code? If yes, then you absolutely know what an *if-statement* is. If not, let's dissect the code now.

On the first line, we declared a variable, `condition`, which is a `string`. Inside our `setup()` function, we set the value of `condition` to `No`. In C, we already have a built-in control statement, known as *if-statement*. Inside our `if()` function, we passed our condition, which is equal to `yes`. The basic syntax for the *if-condition* is as follows:

```
if(condition){
------statements------;
}
```

Inside the curly brackets, we write our statements, which will be executed if the condition inside the `if()` function is true; otherwise, the statement will not be executed. In our example, we passed our `condition` variable's value as *yes*, which is not true because we declared our condition to be `No`. As we stated before, if the condition is false, the statement inside the curly brackets will not be executed.

If we set the `condition` value to `No`, then our statement inside the curly brackets will be executed. In the example, the first if condition is false but the second is true. So, the statement inside the second if will be executed. Let's look at the output of the code:

Yes, our code has the final output **I will not go outside**.

If our block has one statement, we can write the statement directly after the `if()` function. This will not require any curly brackets. Our example can be written as follows:

```
if (condition == "Yes")
Serial.println("I will go outside");
```

But if we have multiple statements, we must place our statements inside the curly brackets. Look at the following example:

```
if(X>Y){
Serial.println("Ha ha ha!");
Serial.println("I knew it");
```

```
Serial.println("X is greater than Y"); }
```

My suggestion is, always use the curly brackets so that you don't need to worry about when to skip brackets or not.

Let's look at another example. Let's say John and Ron are two farmers. They grow flowers. But they are lazy. They hardly take responsibility for selling the flowers. So, they made a pact, which is, if John grows more than 300 flowers, Ron is responsible for selling them. If Ron grows fewer than 200 flowers, John is responsible for selling them. If the number of flowers is the same same, then both will go out selling flowers. One day, John grew 312 flowers and Ron grew 256 flowers. Now, since we know the if condition, let's write a program to find out who will be selling flowers.

First, we need to declare two variables for the number of flowers grown by John and Ron. Let's say they are *jFlower* and *rFlower*. Now, assign the values to them as follows:

```
int jFlower = 312;
int rFlower = 256;
```

You might remember from the previous chapter why we made our variables integers.

Now, let's look at the conditions:

- if jFlower is greater than 300, Ron will be selling the flowers
- if rFlower is less than 200, John will be selling the flowers.
- if jFlower and rFlower are equal, both John and Ron will sell the flowers.

For the three conditions, we need to define three *if-conditions*:

```
//First
if(jFlower > 300){
Serial.println("Ron will sell flower today");
}
//Second
if(rFlower < 200){
Serial.println("John will sell flower today");
}
//Third
if(jFlower == rFlower){
Serial.println("Both John and Ron will sell flower today");
}
```

From the initialization of the two variables (*jFlower* and *rFlower*), we can definitely say which condition will be executed. Let's see if your answer is right. Now, fire up your Arduino IDE and the full code given here:

```
int jFlower = 312;
int rFlower =  256;
void setup() {
  Serial.begin(9600);
  if (jFlower > 300) {
    Serial.println("Ron will sell flower today");
  }
  if (rFlower < 200) {
    Serial.println("John will sell flower today");
  }
  if (jFlower == rFlower) {
    Serial.println("Both John and Ron will sell flower today");
  }

}
void loop() {

}
```

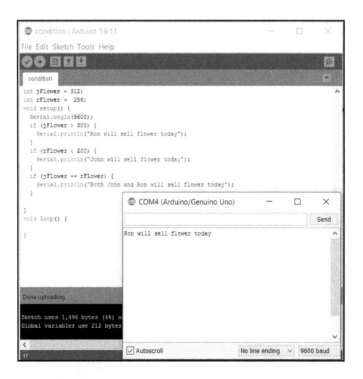

Yes, your answer was right! Ron will be selling flowers today! Let's make the problem even more complex. But before doing that, let's learn about something known as `nested if`.

Nested if

Have you seen a bird's nest? Birds make their nests by collecting leaves, grass, twigs, and so on. But, for most birds, have you noticed they start building the outside of the nest by putting things one over another, and later, they make the nest by surrounding it with small things from inside. Look at the following figure:

`http://tse4.mm.bing.net/th?id=OIP.M9b6c52170fba2232051db1ce4b62b9a7o0`

This is a bird nest made of small, natural objects. There are long leaves both inside the nest and outside the nest, right?

Our nested if is similar to the bird's nest. If an if-statement stays inside another if-statement, the whole structure is known as a nested if-statement. The basic syntax of the nested if looks as follows:

```
if(condition){
--------statements-------
if(condition){
--------statements-------
}
}
```

Remember, there can be multiple if-statements in a nested if. First let's look at the logical operations for a nested if with two if conditions.

Suppose you want to be a member of a club that requires two conditions to be met. You must be over 18 years of age, and you must spend $200 on membership.

If you break any of the two conditions, you cannot have the membership. So, we cannot just use two if conditions. Let's look at what happens if we use a general if-statement other than nested if:

First, we need to declare two variables, as follows:

```
int subscription; //This variable will hold the amount that you want to
spend
int age; // this variable will contain your age.
```

Now we will assign the values. Say, my age is 12 but I want to spend $200 for the membership. See, the subscription amount fulfills the condition of the club, but the age does not. So, the club won't let me be a member of the club. Let's assign values to our variables and write two general if-statements:

```
subscription = 200;
age = 12;
if(subscription ==200){
    Serial.println("You can be our member!");
}
if(age>=18){
    Serial.println("You can be our member!");
}
```

Now, run the code and look at the output:

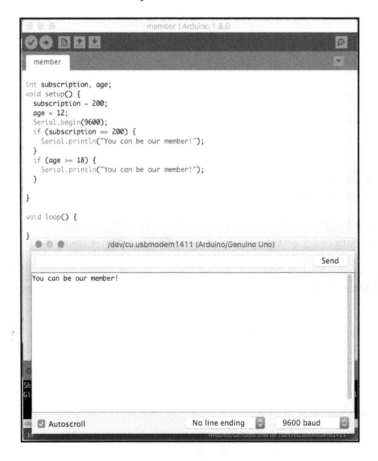

Our output shows only one condition's statement. What happened to the other? It has not been executed due to not being the correct condition. But, we do not want that. We want both the conditions to fulfill the club's requirements so a person can get membership. To check if both the if-statements are executed at the same time, we can use nested if.

If the outer and inner if-statements both fulfill the conditions, our problem can be solved. Let's write the code using nested-if:

```
int subscription;
int age;

void setup() {
  subscription = 200;
  age = 12;
  Serial.begin(9600);
  if (subscription == 200) {
    if (age >= 18) {
      Serial.println("You can be our member!!");
    }
  }

}

void loop() {
}
```

The output looks as follows:

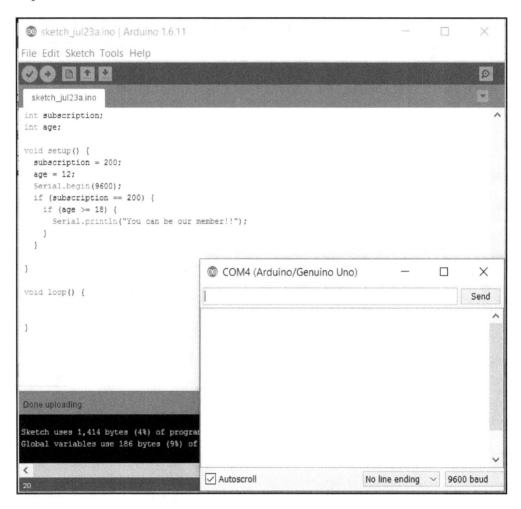

Our output is blank. Why? Because only one condition is fulfilled. If both were true, then we would get the correct result. Let's change the value of age to 30 and run the code again. The output of our code is as follows:

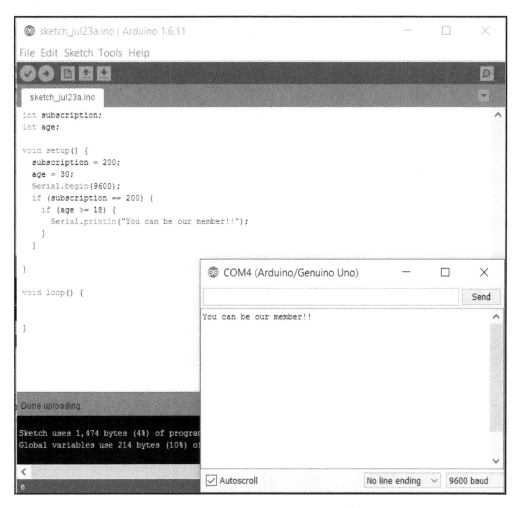

Now our code shows what we expected. Both conditions are fulfilled and we have achieved our desired output.

Can you guess the output of the following code?

```
int subscription;
int age;

void setup() {
  subscription = 250;
  age = 20;
  Serial.begin(9600);
  if (subscription == 200) {
    if (age >= 18) {
      Serial.println("1. You can be our member!!");
    }
  }
  if (subscription == 200) {
    if (age <= 10) {
      Serial.println("2. You can be our member!!");
    }
  }
  if (subscription == 100) {
    if (age >= 18) {
      Serial.println("3. You can be our member!!");
    }
  }
  if (subscription > 100) {
    if (age == 18) {
      Serial.println("4. You can be our member!!");
    }
  }
  if (subscription < 100) {
    if (age > 18) {
      Serial.println("5. You can be our member!!");
    }
  }
  if (subscription > 100) {
    if (age > 10) {
      Serial.println("6. You can be our member!!");
    }
  }
}

void loop() {
}
```

The output is as follows:

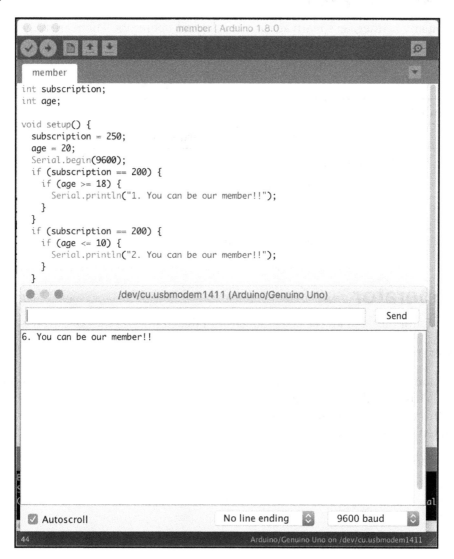

Logical operators

Before going any further, let's learn about a few logical operators. There are only three types of logical operators in C. They are, AND, OR, and NOT. All three operators cover any logical operation. These operators help to remove complexities and shorten the code. Let's learn their symbols first:

Name	Symbol	Meaning
AND	&&	This means, if all the conditions are true, then the condition is true.
OR	||	This means, if any of the conditions are true, then the condition is true.
NOT	!	This operator reverses the condition.

Now we will learn about the operators in detail.

AND operator

The AND operator means if all the conditions fulfill the condition, the condition is true.

Let's look at an example.

Suppose, if today is Monday and the weather is good, I will go to school. See, if both conditions is true, I will do something. But if any of the conditions are false, I won't go to school. In this case, we can either use a nested if or a logical operator inside the if - statement. Let's look at the code.

We first declare two variables:

```
String Day;
String Weather; //it can be a Boolean too. Where true = good and false =
not good
```

Now we set the values of the variables:

```
Day = "Monday";
Weather = "Good";
```

Now we declare an if-statement, where we will use an AND operator:

```
if(Day == "Monday" && Weather == "Good"){
    Serial.println("I will go to school . ");
}
```

If we run the code, we will get *I will go to school* on the console. Do you know why? Because both conditions are true. Still don't believe it? Let's look at the output:

Let's change the value of Day to something else and rerun the code. What do you think? Will there be any output? Yes, you are right. The Serial Monitor will be blank. Let's look at what happens if we change

the value of Day to Sunday:

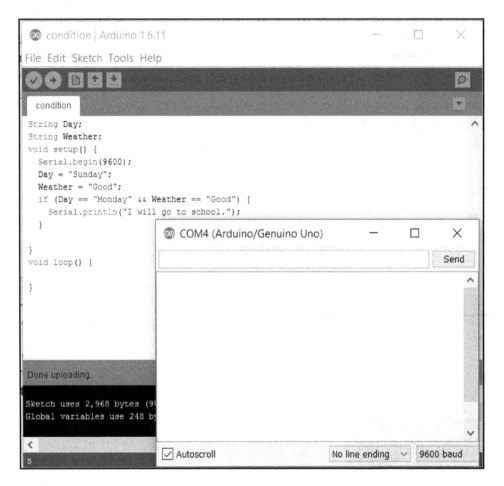

Let's come to a conclusion. The AND operator is used to check if all the conditions are true. If any of the conditions are false, the program will not execute.

Now, check the outputs for the following conditions:

Day	Weather
Monday	Good
Monday	Bad
Friday	Good
Sunday	Good

OR operator

The OR operator means if any of the conditions fulfill the condition, then the condition is true.

Let's look at an example.

If I have a working mouse or a working keyboard, I can play a game. See, I can play the game if either of the devices I have is working. So, our if-statement has two conditions, as before, but with an OR operator, so that if any of the conditions is true, our console shows something. We need to define two variables. This time, let's use two Boolean variables:

```
bool mouse;
bool keyboard;
```

Inside the setup function, declare the variables:

```
mouse = 0; // This means I don't have a mouse. If I had, do you know what I
would write?
keyboard = 1;  //This means I have a keyboard.
```

Let's write our if-statement:

```
If(mouse == 1 || keyboard == 1) {
  Serial.println("You can play the game! ");
}
```

Let's look at the output:

Yes, I can play the game. Now, can you tell me, if I replaced 0 or 1 with `false` and `true`, respectively, would the answer be the same?

How about we change the code as follows and look at the output?

```
bool mouse;
bool keyboard;
void setup() {
  Serial.begin(9600);
```

```
    mouse = false;
    keyboard = true;
    if (mouse == true || keyboard == true) {
      Serial.println("You can play the game");
    }


}
void loop() {

}
```

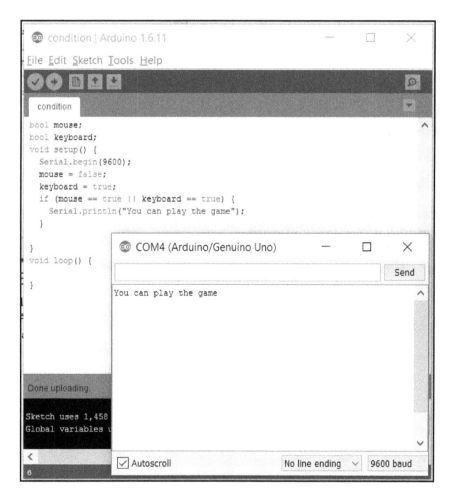

The output is exactly the same as previously. Can you explain why? I guess you know the answer. Can you tell me the output of the same code if our values for the variables were as follows?

Mouse	Keyboard
0	0
0	1
1	0
1	1

NOT operator

The NOT operator inverts the condition. If our condition (only one) is true, our program will not be executed. If false, the program will be executed:

```
If a ==b is true, then !(a==b) is false.
```

Let's look at an example:

1. A peculiar job says you need to be exactly six feet tall to be qualified for the job. If you are not, then you will automatically be disqualified. Let's write a program to check if you are qualified or not.
2. Let's declare a variable first:

```
float height;
```

3. Now assign it to your height:

```
height = 5.11;
```

4. Now write the if-statement:

```
if(height!=6){
    Serial.println("Sorry. You are not qualified.");
}
```

5. So, the full code and output are as follows:

```
float height;
void setup() {
   Serial.begin(9600);
   height = 5.11;
```

```
    if (height != 6) {
        Serial.println("Sorry. You are not qualified!");
    }

}
void loop() {

}
```

Now, check the output for the following inputs of height:

Height	
0	
6	
6.0	
7	
5.99	

If-else

Sometimes our condition has an exception. Say, I will go outside if the weather is good, or I will stay home otherwise. See, something will be done, but if the condition is not met, another thing will be done that is the opposite of the first statement. The basic syntax for the if-else statement is as follows:

```
if (condition) {
   statements //This will be executed if the condition is true
}
else {
   statements //This will be executed if the condition is false
}
```

Let's look at an example:

Ron and Laura are two friends. They went to the mall and bought some pencils. If Ron's number of pencils is greater than Laura's, then Laura will give Ron half of her pencils. Otherwise (else), Ron will give Laura half of his pencils. Find the total number of pencils after all calculations, when Ron buys 130 pencils and Laura buys 146 pencils.

Let's declare two variables for the number of pencils first:

```
int Ron = 130;
int Laura = 146;
Now construct our if-else statements.
   if (Ron > Laura) {
      Serial.println("Ron wins. Ron now has ");
      Serial.print( Ron + Laura / 2);
      Serial.print(" pencils");
   }
   else {
      Serial.println("Laura wins. Laura now has ");
      Serial.print( Laura + Ron / 2);
      Serial.print(" pencils");

   }
```

Fire up the Arduino and run the following full code. You will see the following output:

```
int Ron = 130;
int Laura = 146;
void setup() {
   Serial.begin(9600);
   if (Ron > Laura) {
      Serial.println("Ron wins. Ron now has ");
      Serial.print( Ron + Laura / 2);
```

```
    Serial.print(" pencils");
  }
  else {
    Serial.println("Laura wins. Laura now has ");
    Serial.print( Laura + Ron / 2);
    Serial.print(" pencils");

  }
}
void loop() {

}
```

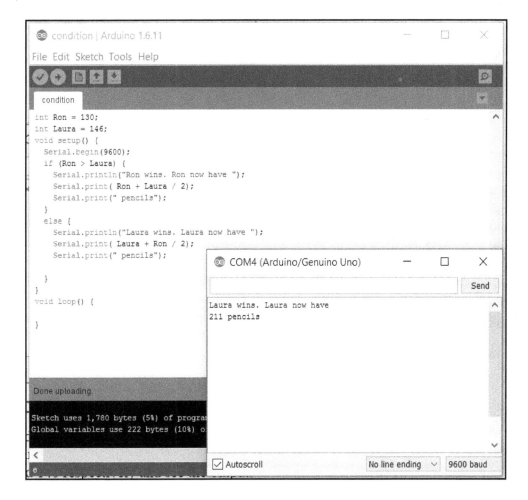

Look at the output. The part inside the `else` was executed. Why? Because the condition was not fulfilled. If the condition was fulfilled, the code inside the else would not be executed. Let's change the values of Ron and Laura to 150 and 140, respectively, and look at the output.

The output will be as follows:

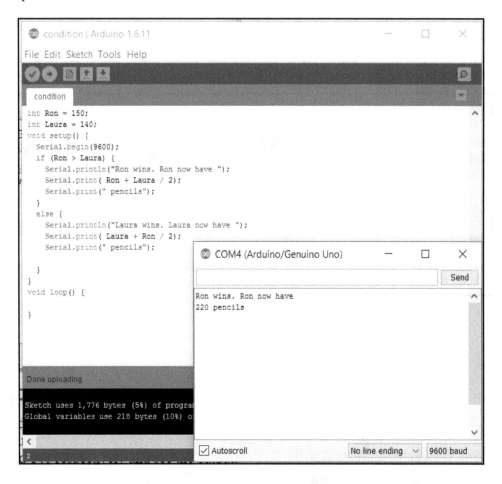

Can you see the difference? This time, Ron has more pencils.

Let's do something more complicated. Say, Ron buys 170 pencils and 168 pens. Laura buys 340 pens and 106 pencils.

Write a program for the following conditions:

- **Case 1**: If Ron has more than 150 pencils and Laura has fewer than 120 pencils, they will share the pencils equally, but not the pens. Otherwise, Ron will own all the pencils. Find out who will have how many pens and pencils.
- **Case 2**: If the total number of pencils is greater than the total number of pens, Ron will buy all the pens; if not, Laura will buy all the pencils. If the first condition is true, there is another condition: if the sum of pens and pencils of one individual is greater than the other's, the person who has more will have to buy 100 pencils from the other. Find the number of pens and pencils Ron and Laura each have.

For the first case, we need to define a few variables, as follows:

```
int RPencils = 170, RPens = 168, LPencils = 106, LPens =340;
```

Now construct out conditions as follows:

```
if (RPencils > 150 && LPencils < 120) {
    Serial.println("Ron and Laura both have ");
    Serial.print((RPencils + LPencils) / 2);
    Serial.print(" pencils");
    Serial.println("And Ron has ");
    Serial.print(RPens);
    Serial.print(" pens, ");
    Serial.println(" And Laura has ");
    Serial.print(LPens);
    Serial.print(" pens, ");
  }
  else {
    Serial.print("Ron has ");
    Serial.print(RPencils + LPencils);
    Serial.print(" pencils. And");
    Serial.print(RPens);
    Serial.print(" pens. ");
    Serial.print("Laura has no pencil but");
    Serial.print(RPens);
    Serial.print(" pens");
  }
```

Can you say which part of the code will be executed? Yes, the if part. Because both the conditions inside the if part are `true`. So, the output will be as follows:

Change the values of `LPencils` to 130 and look at the result. The output will be as follows:

Can you tell why the *else* part executed? Yes, because one of the conditions inside the `if` part was not true.

Let's move to the second case. For this case, our variables will remain the same as the first case. We can see that we will need an `if-else` statement. But the if-statement will contain another if-statement, right? Let's write the conditions:

```
if ((RPencils + LPencils) > (RPens + LPens)) {
  Serial.print("Ron buys Laura's pen and he has ");
  Serial.print(RPens + LPens);
```

```
    Serial.println(" pens");
    if ((RPens + RPencils) > (LPens + LPencils)) {
      Serial.println("Ron will buy Laura 100 pencils");
    }
    else {
      Serial.println("Laura will buy Ron 100 pencils");
    }
  }
  else {
    Serial.print("Laura buys Ron's pencils and she has ");
    Serial.print(RPencils + LPencils);
    Serial.print(" pencils");
  }
```

Can you tell the output from the code? I hope you can. Let's look at the output:

Yes, the else part was executed! Can you set the variables so that the if part executes?

Switch-case

If we have multiple conditions, we sometimes use `switch-case` for the simplicity of the logic. The basic structure of `switch-case` is as follows:

```
switch (expression) {
case constant-expression  :
   statement;
   break;
case constant-expression  :
   statement;
   break;
   //more cases
default :
   statement;
}
```

Here, by expression, we mean the variable itself. constant-expression denotes the value of the condition. We have to write break after every case to avoid the execution of the next case statements. If none of the cases match the expression, the default case executes. The default case does not need to have a break. Let's look at an example.

Mary bakes cakes. She codes her cakes as follows, for a quick response to her customers:

- 101 is Layer cake
- 102 is Lamington cake
- 103 is Lady Baltimore cake
- 104 is Apple cake
- 105 is Coconut cake
- 106 is Frog cake
- 107 is Madeira cake
- 108 is Rum cake
- 109 is Strawberry cake
- 110 is Welsh cake

The customer types the code number and Mary takes the order. Write a program that will contain the customer's order. If the code doesn't match any of the codes, the customer will get an error message.

Declare an integer variable, customer, and assign 105 to it:

```
int customer = 105;
```

Now write the switch-case for our problem. The full code is as follows:

```
int customer = 105 ;
void setup() {
  Serial.begin(9600);

  switch (customer) { //We will check customer's value
    case 101:
      Serial.print("Layer cake");
      break;
    case 102:
      Serial.print("Lamington");
      break;
    case 103:
      Serial.print("Lady Baltimore cake");
      break;
    case 104:
      Serial.print("Apple cake");
      break;
    case 105:
      Serial.print("Coconut cake");
      break;
    case 106:
      Serial.print("Frog cake");
      break;
    case 107:
      Serial.print("Madeira cake");
      break;
    case 108:
      Serial.print("Rum cake");
      break;
    case 109:
      Serial.print("Strawberry cake");
      break;
    case 110:
      Serial.print("Welsh cake");
      break;
  deafult: //If no case is true
      Serial.print("Error! Please enter a correct code! ");
   }
 }
 void loop() {
 }
```

The output of the code is as follows:

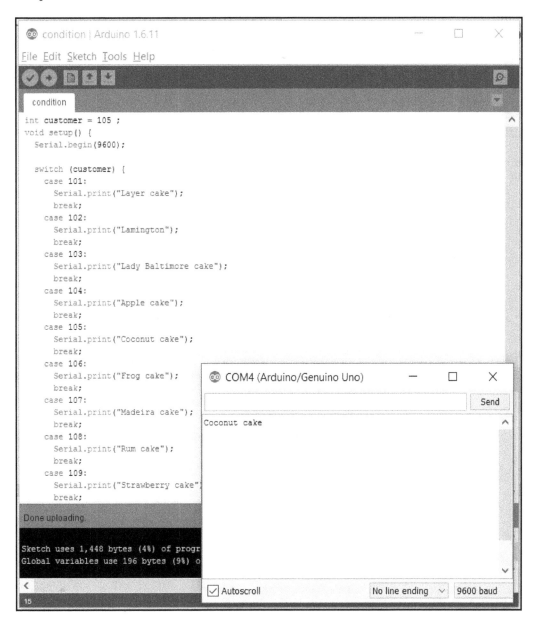

Now change the values to customer, as follows, and check your outputs:

Customer
100
104
106
00
201

Let's do another program. We will find out the largest of three integers.

Let's declare three variables and assign integer numbers to them, as follows:

```
int a = 10;
int b = 20;
int c = 30;
```

We will use if, if-else, and nested if to find the largest number.

With an if-statement, we can use the following code. Don't worry, I'll explain it soon:

```
if (a >= b && a >= c)
{
  Serial.print(a);
  Serial.print(" is the largest number");
}

if (b >= a && b >= c) {
  Serial.print(b);
  Serial.print(" is the largest number");
}

if (c >= a && c >= b)
{
  Serial.print(c);
  Serial.print(" is the largest number");
}
```

The logic is simple. If *a* is greater than both *b* and *c*, then *a* is the largest. If *b* is greater than both *a* and *c*, then *b* is the largest. If *c* is greater than both *a* and *b*, then *c* is the largest. Finally, we found the largest number, which is 30. Let's look at the output:

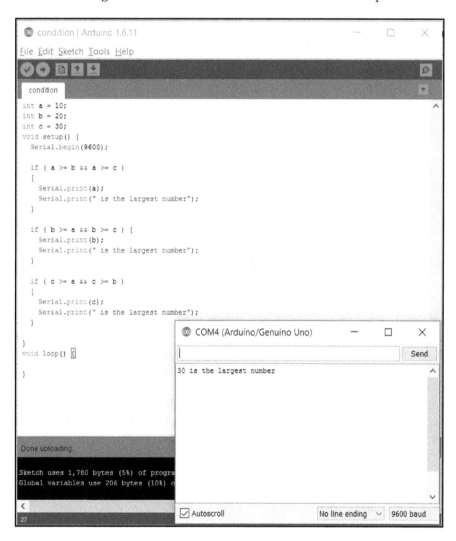

Let's see whether `if-else` gives the same result. The main code should be as follows:

```
if (a >= b)
{
  if (a >= c) {
    Serial.print(a);
    Serial.print(" is the largest");
  }
  else {
    Serial.print(c);
    Serial.println(" is the largest.");
  }
}
else
{
  if (b >= c) {
    Serial.print(b);
    Serial.println(" is the largest.");
  }
  else {
    Serial.print(c);
    Serial.println(" is the largest.");
  }
}
```

We used one main `if-else` statement, and inside the if, we added the condition, if *a* is greater than or equal to *b*. If the condition is fulfilled, there is another `if-else` statement, where the if has the condition, if *a* is greater than or equal to *c*. If this is fulfilled, then we would say *a* is the largest; else, *c* is the largest. The *else* part of the first if executes when the first if is not true. Inside the *else*, we have another `if-else`, which will be executed if *a* is not greater than or equal to *b*. Inside the else, the first if has the condition: if *b* is greater than or equal to *c*, then *b* is the largest; else, *c* is the largest. Let's look at the output to check if our code is right:

Yes, our output is the same.

Now we will use a slightly different thing, called `else-if`, to find the largest number.

The main part of the code will be as follows:

```
if ( a >= b && a >= c) {
    Serial.print(a);
    Serial.print(" is the largest");

}
else {
    if (b >= a && b >= c) {
        Serial.print(b);
        Serial.print(" is the largest");

    }
    else {
        Serial.print(c);
        Serial.print(" is the largest");
    }
}
```

We used an `if-else` statement. Inside the *else* part, we used another `if-else` statement. If the conditions inside the outer `if` do not fulfill, the else part will be executed. Inside the outer `if`, we said, if *a* is greater than or equal to *b* and *a* is greater than or equal to *c*, then a is the largest number. Inside the *else* part, we have another if that has the condition, if b is greater than or equal to *a* and *b* is greater than or equal to *c*. If the condition is true, then *b* is the largest; else *c* is the largest. Let's look at the output:

Yes! The output is the same. Can you tell which of the algorithms is easy to use and why? Now let's do thane exercise to sharpen your learning.

Exercises

- Write a program to check if a number is odd or even (hint: find the modulus of the number by 2, and if the modulus is equal to 1, then the number is even; else the number is odd).
- Take inputs of three variables (Name, Age, and Email) from a user. If the age is greater than 20, print all the variables. If the age is equal to or less than 20, print "Sorry! You are not allowed!".
- Take an input of three integers and print the largest integer (hint: follow the previous example)
- Take the input of the marks of a student (four subjects) and find his GPA (hint: take variables as float; use if conditions to find the GPA of a subject; then add all the GPAs, divide the total with the total number of subjects, and print the value).
- Define the days of a week from 1 to 7. Take an input of the day number, and if the day number is odd, print "Have a lovely day;" if the day number is even, print "It is a lovely day!"

Loops

Loop executes a sequence of statements until a specific condition is true. Loops help to do things again and again according to the conditions. In programming, we use loops if we need to do the same thing multiple times. There are basically three types of loops in C for Arduino. They are as follows:

- `for` loop
- `while` loop
- `do-while` loop

Each loop has its own structure, but one thing is common to all of them: each loop needs a condition to control the loop. Let's look at the *for* loop first.

for loop

The `for` loop has four major parts. They are as follows:

- Initialization
- Condition

- Increment/Decrement
- Statements

The **initialization** means assigning initial values to a variable. The condition controls the loop in terms of how many times the loop will run. The increment/decrements operator means increasing, decreasing, or changing the value of the variable until it matches the condition. The basic syntax of a for loop is as follows:

```
for (initialization; conditions; increment/decrement)
{
        // statements
}
```

The flowchart of the for loop is as follows:

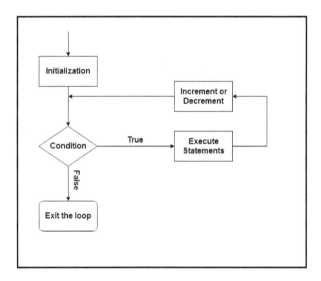

Let's look at an example.

You want to print Hello World five times on the Serial Monitor. You can print it by writing five serial print statements, or five times in a single serial print statement. But if you needed to print Hello World 1,000 times, will you write 1,000 lines? I doubt it. In that case, a loop can help you. So, for a loop, we need a *driver variable* for the loop, which will maintain the loop.

We want to print "Hello World" five times, so our condition is to run the loop five times, right? Then we will break the loop. First, we need to initialize the *driver variable*. Then we will increase the value of the variable by 1 each time, until its value is 5. Declare a variable first. This time, we are taking an integer variable:

```
int driver;
```

Now write our *for loop* with the following syntax:

```
for (driver = 1; driver <= 5; driver = driver + 1) {
  //statement
}
```

This loop will start from 1 and increase the value of the variable by 1 each time, until the condition is false; that is, the value of driver becomes greater than 5.

Our increment is by 1, so we wrote `driver = driver+1`. We could also write `driver++`, which would mean the same.

Our code will run five times. The compiler will look at the initialization first. Then it will look at the condition. If the condition is `true`, the statements inside the loop will be executed. Then it will return to the increment/decrement part, make the change to the state of the driver variable, and then look at the condition. If the condition is again true, the statements will be executed. The same thing will happen until the condition is `true`. Our code to print `Hello World` five times may look as follows:

```
int driver;
void setup() {
  Serial.begin(9600);
  for (driver = 1; driver <= 5; driver = driver + 1) {
    Serial.println("Hello World");
  }

}
void loop() {

}
```

The output will look as follows:

We got `Hello World` five times. This is what we wanted. Now, can you tell me what our code would be if we wanted to write 100 lines of Hello World?

Yes, we only need to change the condition to `driver<=100`. The rest of the code remains same.

Let's print the following series using a loop:

2,4,6,8,10,12,14,16,18,20............................100

You can see that the series started from 2 and incremented by 2. So, our loop would be as follows, where *i* is an integer-type variable:

```
for (i = 2; i <= 100; i = i + 2) {
}
```

Inside the loop, all we need to print the value is *i*. Let's look at the full code and output:

```
int i;

void setup() {
  Serial.begin(9600);
  for (i = 2; i <= 100; i = i + 2) {
    Serial.println(i);
  }


}
void loop() {
}
```

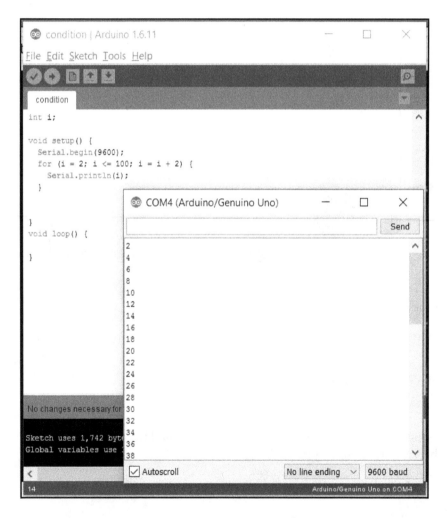

Yes, the output is showing what we wanted!

Can you tell me what we have to do inside the loop if we want exactly the same format of the loop (2,4,6,8,10………)?

The print function would be as follows:

```
Serial.print(i);
Serial.print(",");
```

We need to print both the functions; then our output would be what we want. Want to see the output? Here it is:

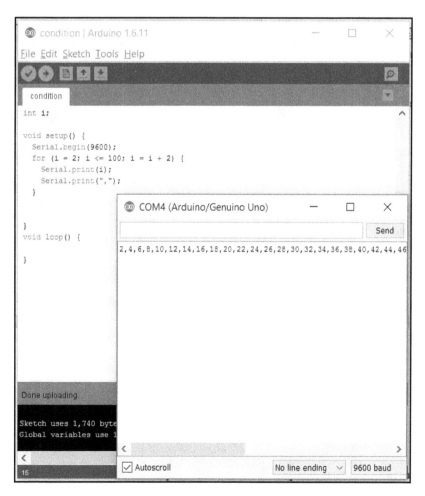

Let's do something in descending order. We will print the following series:

```
100, 95, 90, 85,80,75,70.............................0
```

Our loop starts from 100. So, the initialization is 100, and this will continue until the driver variable reaches 0; we need to decrease, and the decrease is by 5, right? The loop will look as follows, where *i* is the driver operator:

```
for(i = 100; i >= 0; i = i - 5) {
    Serial.print(i);
    Serial.print(",");
}
```

The output of the code is as follows:

Nested for loop

A nested for loop is similar to the nested if, except the continues running of a statement. In a nested for loop, the loop inside the first for completes for a single execution of the outer loop. Say our loop runs five times until the condition is false. Inside this loop, we now add another loop that runs three times, until the condition is `false`. So, for each execution of the outer loop, the inner loop will run three times, right? In total, the whole thing will run 5×3=15 times. You can calculate the total execution with a simple calculation:

```
Total expectations = P x Q
```

Here, P = The number of times the outer loop runs, and Q = The number of times the inner loop runs.

If we have more loops in the nest, we need to multiply execution time with it to get the total number of executions.

Let's look at an example.

Let's draw the following shape using a for loop:

```
* * * * *
* * * * *
* * * * *
* * * * *
```

The shape has five stars in each row, and four rows. So, the outer loop should run four times, where the inner loop should run five times. Inside the inner loop, we need to print a star; then we will get the output. Let's construct our nested loop, where i and j are the driver variables:

```
for (i = 0; i < 4; i++ ) {
   for (j = 0; j < 5; j++) {
      Serial.print("*");
   }
}
```

Do you think this nested loop will print what we want? Our condition for the first loop starts from 0 and ends when the driver variable is equal to 4:

- for 0, our loop is valid
- for 1, our loop is valid
- for 2, our loop is valid
- for 3, our loop is valid
- for 4, our loop is invalid

We can see that our loop runs four times. So, there is no problem in the code. The inner for loop will run five times for the same reason, right?

Let's look at the output of our code:

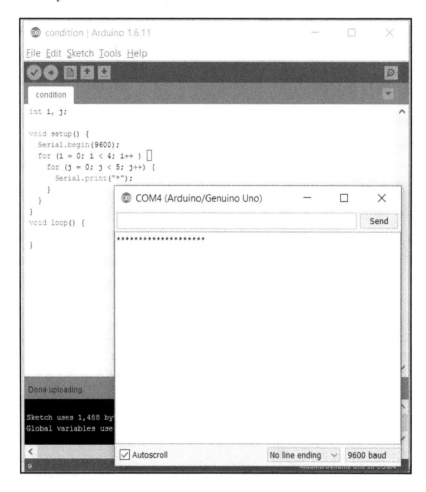

No, we did not want that output. We wanted a new line after five stars printed. So, we need to print a new line after the inner loop finishes running once. Look at the following code:

```
int i, j;

void setup() {
  Serial.begin(9600);
  for (i = 0; i < 4; i++ ) {
    for (j = 0; j < 5; j++) {
      Serial.print ("*");
```

```
    }
    Serial.print("\n"); //for new line.
  }
}
void loop() {

}
```

Let's look at the output now:

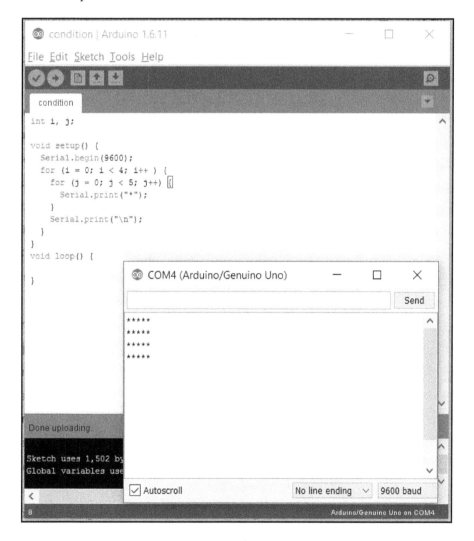

Yes. Now we have what we wanted!

Let's learn about another type of loop.

While loop

A `while` loop is almost the same as a for loop. The basic syntax of a while loop is as follows:

```
while (condition) {
   //Statements.
}
```

The algorithm of a while loop is shown in the following figure:

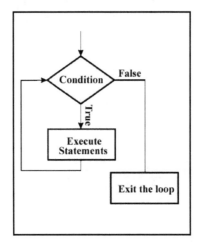

It's easy to use. Say we want to print 1-10 using a while loop. We can do it as follows:

```
int i = 1;
   while (i <= 10) {
      Serial.println(i);
      i++;
   }
```

We also need to initialize the driver variable in the while loop. In the for loop, we initialized inside the for loop, but in a while loop, we need to initialize it before writing the while loop, as we did for the preceding code. We also incremented the value of the driver variable by one just before the while loop is about to end. This task depends on the purpose of the code. Let's look at the output of the code:

Let's convert the nested `for loop` for the shape we printed previously. The converted code will look as follows. See the comments for clarification:

```
int i,j; //declared driver variables

void setup() {
  Serial.begin(9600);
```

```
    i=0; //initialized first driver variable
    while (i < 4) {
      j = 0; //initialized second driver variable
      while (j < 5) {
        Serial.print("*");
        j++; //incremented 2nd loop's driver variable
      }
      Serial.print("\n");
      i++; //incremented 1st loop's driver variable
    }
}
void loop() {

}
```

Let's look at the output:

The output looks exactly like the previous shape. For a nested `while loop`, you need to remember to refresh your driver variable just before using it on the loop. That is, you need to initialize your driver variable just before each while loop starts. Let's learn about the last type of loop.

do-while loop

A *do-while* loop is a modified version of a *while* loop. The syntax of the `do-while` loop is as follows:

```
do {
    //statement
} while(condition);
```

In other loops, the statement does not execute if the condition is not true, but in a do-while loop, the statement will be executed at least once, even though the condition is false.

The flowchart of a `do-while` loop is as follows:

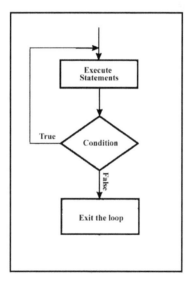

Look at the following code, and carefully read the comments to see what happened inside the code:

```
int i = 1; //initialized the variable

void setup() {
  Serial.begin(9600);
```

```
    do {
       Serial.print ("Hello World"); //The do part will be executed
    }
    while (i > 10); //The condition is false, right?
}
void loop() {

}
```

Our do-while loop has two parts. The do part executed even though the condition was false (we initialized i=1, and the condition says that if the value of I is greater than 10, the loop will be valid). So, our code will show **Hello World** only once.

Now look at the output:

Exercise

Using a loop, draw the following shapes:

a.

```
*
* *
* * *
* * * *
* * * * *
* * * * * *
```

b.

```
* * * * * *
* * * * *
* * * *
* * *
* *
*
```

c.

```
11
1111
111111
11111111
```

Summary

In this chapter, we have learned about a lot of things, including control statements (if-else, loops, switch, and so on). All the control statements we learned are equally important for the next level of Arduino programming. This chapter might be a long one, but my suggestion is that you read the whole chapter without stopping. You should also do the exercises so that your learning remains in your brain for a long time. If you have any problems understanding any code or topic, then you will not be quite ready for the next chapter, where we will learn a lot of interesting things, including file handling and functions. If you are already familiar with all the topics of this chapter, you are most welcome to move onto the next Chapter 5, *Functions and Files with Arduino*.

5
Functions and Files with Arduino

In this chapter, we will learn about functions and file handling with Arduino. In the previous chapter, we learned about loops and conditions, which will be used in this chapter too. If you skipped the previous chapter, I would suggest you go through it, and come back to this chapter later. Let's begin out journey into Functions and Files with Arduino.

Functions

Do you know how to make instant coffee? Don't worry; I know. You will need some water, instant coffee, sugar, and milk or creamer. Remember, we want to drink coffee, but we are doing something that makes coffee. This procedure can be defined as a function of coffee making. Let's finish making coffee now. The steps can be written as follows:

1. Boil some water.
2. Put some coffee inside a mug.
3. Add some sugar.
4. Pour in boiled water.
5. Add some milk.

And finally, your coffee is ready! Let's write a pseudo code for this function:

```
function coffee (water, coffee, sugar, milk) {
  add coffee beans;
  add sugar;
  pour boiled water;
  add milk;
```

```
    return coffee;
}
```

In our pseudo code we have four items (we would call them parameters) to make coffee. We did something with our ingredients, and finally, we got our coffee, right? Now, if anybody wants to get coffee, he/she will have to do the same function (in programming, we will call it calling a function) again. Let's move into the types of functions.

Types of functions

A function returns something, or a value, which is called the **return** value. The return values can be of several types, some of which are listed here:

- Integers
- Float
- Double
- Character
- Void
- Boolean

Another term, **argument**, refers to something that is passed to the function and calculated or used inside the function. In our previous example, the ingredients passed to our coffee-making process can be called arguments (sugar, milk, and so on), and we finally got the coffee, which is the return value of the function.

By definition, there are two types of functions. They are, a **system-defined** function and a **user-defined** function. In our Arduino code, we have often seen the following structure:

```
void setup() {
}
void loop() {
}
```

setup() and loop() are also functions. The return type of these functions is void. Don't worry, we will discuss the type of function soon. The setup() and loop() functions are system-defined functions. There are a number of system-defined functions. The user-defined functions cannot be named after them.

Before going deeper into function types, let's learn the syntax of a function. Functions can be as follows:

```
void functionName()
{
    //statements
}
Or like
void functionName(arg1, arg2, arg3)
{
    //statements
}
```

So, what's the difference? Well, the first function has no arguments, but the second function does.

There are four types of function, depending on the return type and arguments. They are as follows:

- A function with no arguments and no return value
- A function with no arguments and a return value
- A function with arguments and no return value
- A function with arguments and a return value

Now, the question is, can the arguments be of any type? Yes, they can be of any type, depending on the function. They can be Boolean, integers, floats, or characters. They can be a mixture of data types too. We will look at some examples later. Now, let's define and look at examples of the four types of function we just defined.

Function with no arguments and no return value, these functions do not accept arguments. The return type of these functions is void, which means the function returns nothing. Let me clear this up. As we learned earlier, a function must be named by something. The naming of a function will follow the rule for the variable naming. If we have a name for a function, we need to define its type also. It's the basic rule for defining a function. So, if we are not sure of our function's type (what type of job it will do), then it is safe to use the void keyword in front of our function, where void means no data type, as in the following function:

```
void myFunction(){
//statements
}
```

Inside the function, we may do all the things we need. Say we want to print I love Arduino! 10 times if the function is called. So, our function must have a loop that continues for ten times and then stops. So, our function can be written as follows:

```
void myFunction() {
  int i;

  for (i = 0; i < 10; i++) {
    Serial.println("I love Arduino!");
  }
}
```

The preceding function does not have a return value. But if we call the function from our main function (from the setup() function; we may also call it from the loop() function, unless we do not want an infinite loop), the function will print I love Arduino! 10 times. No matter how many times we call, it will print 10 times for each call.

Let's write the full code and look at the output. The full code is as follows:

```
void myFunction() {
  int i;

  for (i = 0; i < 10; i++) {
    Serial.println("I love Arduino!");
  }
}
void setup() {
  Serial.begin(9600);
  myFunction(); // We called our function
  Serial.println("................"); //This will print some dots
  myFunction(); // We called our function again
}

void loop() {
  // put your main code here, to run repeatedly:

}
```

In the code, we placed our function (myFunction) after the loop() function. It is a good practice to declare the custom function before the setup() loop. Inside our setup() function, we called the function, then printed a few dots, and finally, we called our function again. You can guess what will happen. Yes, I love Arduino! will be printed 10 times, then a few dots will be printed, and finally, I love Arduino! will be printed 10 times. Let's look at the output on the serial monitor:

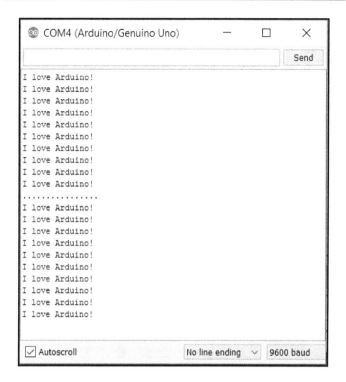

Yes. Your assumption is correct!

Functions with no arguments and a return value

In this type of function, no arguments are passed, but they return a value. You need to remember that the return value depends on the type of the function. If you declare a function as an integer function, the return value's type will have to have be an integer also. If you declare a function as a character, the return type must be a character. This is true for all other data types as well.

Let's look at an example. We will declare an integer function, where we will define a few integers. We will add them and store them to another integer, and finally, return the addition. The function may look as follows:

```
int addNum() {
  int a = 3, b = 5, c = 6, addition;
  addition = a + b + c;
  return addition;
}
```

The preceding function should return 14. Let's store the function's return value to another integer type of variable in the setup() function and print in on the serial monitor.

The full code will be as follows:

```
void setup() {
  Serial.begin(9600);
  int fromFunction = addNum(); // added values to an integer
  Serial.println(fromFunction); // printed the integer
}

void loop() {

}

int addNum() {
  int a = 3, b = 5, c = 6, addition; //declared some integers
  addition = a + b + c; // added them and stored into another integers
  return addition; // Returned the addition.
}
```

The output will look as follows:

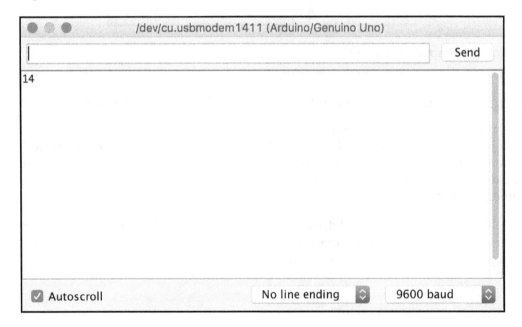

Function with arguments and no return value

This type of function processes some arguments inside the function, but does not return anything directly. We can do the calculations inside the function, or print something, but there will be no return value.

Say we need find out the sum of two integers. We may define a number of variables to store them, and then print the sum. But with the help of a function, we can just pass two integers through a function; then, inside the function, all we need to do is sum them and store them in another variable. Then we will print the value. Every time we call the function and pass our values through it, we will get the sum of the integers we pass. Let's define a function that will show the sum of the two integers passed through the function. We will call the function `sumOfTwo()`, and since there is no return value, we will define the function as void. The function should look as follows:

```
void sumOfTwo(int a, int b) {
   int sum = a + b;
   Serial.print("The sum is " );
   Serial.println(sum);
}
```

Whenever we call this function with proper arguments, the function will print the sum of the number we pass through the function. Let's look at the output first; then we will discuss the code:

We pass the arguments to a function, separating them with commas. The sequence of the arguments must not be messed up while we call the function. Because the arguments of a function may be of different types, if we mess up while calling, the program may not compile and will not execute correctly:

Say a function looks as follows:

```
void myInitialAndAge(int age, char initial) {
   Serial.print("My age is ");
   Serial.println(age);
   Serial.print("And my initial is ");
   Serial.print(initial);
}
```

Now, we must call the function like so: `myInitialAndAge(6,'T');`, where 6 is my age and T is my initial. We should not do it as follows: `myInitialAndAge('T', 6);`:

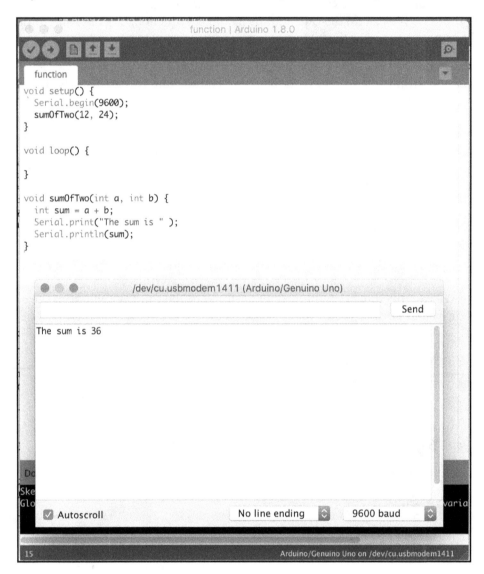

We called the function and passed two values through it (12 and 24). We got the output as **The sum is 36**. Isn't it amazing? Let's go a little bit deeper. In our function, we declared our two arguments (*a* and *b*) as integers. Inside the whole function, the values (12 and 24) we passed through the function are as follows:

```
a = 12 and b =24;
```

If we called the function this `sumOfTwo(24, 12)`, the values of the variables would be as follows:

```
a = 24 and b = 12;
```

I hope you can now understand the sequence of arguments of a function. How about an experiment? Call the `sumOfTwo()` function five times in the `setup()` function, with different values of a and b, and compare the outputs.

Functions with arguments and a return value

This type of function will have both the arguments and the return value. Inside the function, there will be some processing or calculations using the arguments, and later, there would be an outcome, which we want as a return value. Since this type of function will return a value, the function must have a type. Let's look at an example.

We will write a function that will check if a number is prime or not. From your math class, you may remember that a prime number is a natural number greater than 1 that has no positive divisors other than 1 and itself.

The basic logic behind checking whether a number is prime or not is to check all the numbers starting from 2 to the number before the number itself by dividing the number. Not clear? Ok, let's check if 9 is a prime number. No, it is not a prime number. Why? Because it can be divided by 3. And according to the definition, the prime number cannot be divisible by any number other than 1 and the number itself.

So, we will check if 9 is divisible by 2. No, it is not. Then we will divide by 3 and yes, it is divisible. So, 9 is not a prime number, according to our logic. Let's check if 13 is a prime number. We will check if the number is divisible by 2, 3, 4, 5, 6, 7, 8, 9, 10, 11, and 12. No, the number is not divisible by any of those numbers. We may also shorten our checking by only checking the number that is half of the number we are checking. Look at the following code:

```
int primeChecker(int n) // n is our number which will be checked
{
    int i; // Driver variable for the loop
```

```
    for (i = 2; i <= n / 2; i++) // Continued the loop till n/2
    {
      if (n % i == 0) // If no reminder
        return 1; // It is not prime
    }

    return 0; // else it is prime
  }
```

The code is quite simple. If the remainder is equal to zero, our number is fully divisible by a number other than 1 and itself, so it is not a prime number. If there is any remainder, the number is a prime number. Let's write the full code and look at the output for the following numbers:

```
23
65
235
4,543
4,241
```

The full source code to check if the numbers are prime or not is as follows:

```
void setup() {
  Serial.begin(9600);
  primeChecker(23); // We called our function passing our number to test.
  primeChecker(65);
  primeChecker(235);
  primeChecker(4543);
  primeChecker(4241);
}

void loop() {
}

int primeChecker(int n)
{
  int i; //driver variable for the loop

  for (i = 2; i <= n / 2; ++i) //loop continued until the half of the
numebr
  {
    if (n % i == 0)
      return Serial.println("Not a prime number"); // returned the number
status
  }

  return Serial.println("A prime number");
}
```

This is a very simple code. We just called our `primeChecker()` function and passed our numbers. Inside our `primeChecker()` function, we wrote the logic to check our number. Now let's look at the output:

From the output, we can see that, other than 23 and 4,241, none of the numbers are prime.

Let's look at an example, where we will write four functions: add(), sub(), mul(), and divi(). Into these functions, we will pass two numbers, and print the value on the serial monitor. The four functions can be defined as follows:

```
float sum(float a, float b) {
    float sum = a + b;
    return sum;
}

float sub(float a, float b) {
    float sub = a - b;
    return sub;
}
float mul(float a, float b) {
    float mul = a * b;
    return mul;
}
float divi(float a, float b) {
    float divi = a / b;
    return divi;
}
```

Now write the rest of the code, which will give the following outputs:

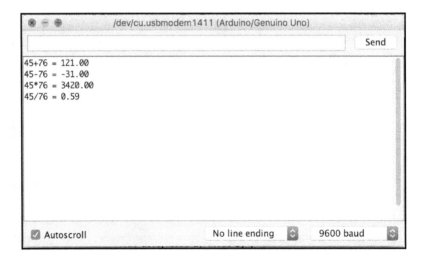

Usages of functions

You may wonder which type of function we should use. The answer is simple. The usages of the functions are dependent on the operations of the programs. But whatever the function is, I would suggest to do only a single task with a function. Do not do multiple tasks inside a function. This will usually speed up your processing time and the calculation time of the code.

You may also want to know why we even need to use functions. Well, there a number of uses of functions, as follows:

- Functions help programmers write more organized code
- Functions help to reduce errors by simplifying code
- Functions make the whole code smaller
- Functions create an opportunity to use the code multiple times

Exercise

To extend your knowledge of functions, you may want to do the following exercise:

- Write a program to check if a number is even or odd. (Hint: you may remember the % operator).
- Write a function that will find the largest number among four numbers. The numbers will be passed as arguments through the function. (Hint: use if-else conditions).
- Suppose you work in a garment factory. They need to know the area of a cloth. The area can be in float. They will provide you the length and height of the cloth. Now write a program using functions to find out the area of the cloth. (Use basic calculation in the user-defined function).

Data logging

Our next topic concerns connecting an SD card to our Arduino board and reading data from the SD card. We will also learn how to write data to the SD card. Before learning reading or writing, we need to know about data logging. In Arduino, we can connect sensors, and sensors can sense *something*. For instance, a humidity sensor can measure the humidity in the air, or a temperature sensor can determine the temperature of the environment. All the information from the sensors comes to the Arduino as the fluctuation of a few numbers (usually voltage). We will discuss sensors later. Our point is, the numbers sometimes need to be stored. Let's imagine we need to measure the humidity of different locations and collect data from at least 500 places. We don't want to go to 500 places with our Arduino board connected to the PC. Other than uploading the code and visualizing the output, an Arduino can be used alone. We can connect an SD card and the sensors to the Arduino, and power it with a portable battery. Then we can move to 500 places easily. In this process, we will get data from any number of places without causing much trouble. The process of data collection is called data logging.

File handling

Handling files with Arduino is challenging. We will learn how to read and write files using Arduino Uno. By file handling, we mean creating a file, modifying a file, and deleting a file. The **FILE** keyword is used to declare a temporary variable with which the data of a file can be stored and later modified.

Connecting an SD card to your Arduino

Let's move on to an interesting subject. We will now connect an SD card to our Arduino, read files from it, and write a file to the card. To connect an SD card to your Arduino, you need an SD card module. So, what is an SD card module? Alright, an SD card module is an extended part of Arduino which can be added to read or write an SD card. There are two types of card module in the market, an SD card module and a micro SD card module. In this chapter, we will use the a micro SD card module.

Following is a photo of different SD card modules:

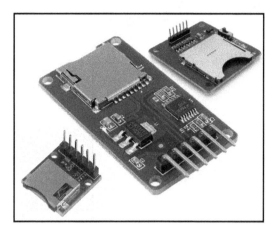

Now you can clearly understand what an SD card module is. It's much like a card reader, but slightly different. Most SD card modules have six pins in common. The pin out of the module is as shown in the following photo:

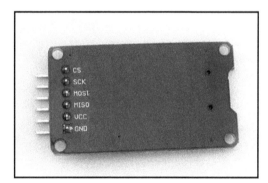

So, you may be wondering what the pins do. Okay, before learning about the card module pins, let's learn about our memory cards' pins. We usually use SD or micro SD cards. Usually, an SD card has 9 pins and a micro SD card has 8 pins. Let's name the pins of the cards, as follows:

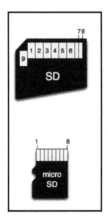

The names of the pins for the SD card are listed in the following table:

Pin number	Pin name
1	CD/DATA3
2	CMD
3	VSS
4	VDD
5	CLK
6	VSS2
7	DATA0
8	DATA1
9	DATA2

The names of the pins for the micro SD card are listed in the following table:

Pin number	Pin name
1	DATA2
2	CD/DATA3
3	CMD
4	VDD
5	CLK
6	VSS
7	DATA0
8	DATA1

To read and write to the card, we will only use six pins. The pin out of the card module shown in the preceding photo shows the following pin names:

Pin Name	Meaning
CS/SS	Select Slave
SCK	Serial Clock
MOSI	Master Out, Slave In
MISO	Master In, Slave Out
VCC/5V	Power Pin (5 volts/3.3volts)
GND	Ground Pin

Now we will need a micro SD card. Before connecting the SD card to the module, make sure it is formatted. The format type should be either FAT16 or FAT32, because our Arduino library for SD card can only read these formats.

Formatting the SD/Micro SD card

To format the card, you need to connect the card to your PC with a card reader (or any electronic device; our main target is to see the card on the PC and format it):

- **Formatting on Windows**: Formatting an SD/Micro SD card on a Windows PC is super simple. In the explorer, right-click on the card and click format. Make sure you select the format type as either FAT16 or FAT32.
- **Formatting on Linux**: Go to Terminal and type *df*. You'll see the names of the drives connected to the PC. The names will be as follows: /dev/sdb1. Make sure it is your SD card, then type the following command and hit Enter:

```
sudo mkdosfs -F 16 /dev/sdb1
```

Here, sdb1 should be replaced with your SD card's name:

- **Formatting on OSX**: Open Disk Utility (Go to Finder, select Applications, and select Utilities; you'll find Disk Utility). Choose your card from the left-hand side and choose *Erase* from the top. Select **MS-DOS (FAT)** from the options. You may find a few hidden files after formatting the SD card on OSX. It's not a big deal. After formatting, the card name will be changed. You can rename it anytime. You can also use Terminal in OSX to format the SD card. Just type the following commands in Terminal and hit Enter:

  ```
  newfs_msdos -F 16 (path to SD Card device)/(SD Card device
  number)
  ```
  Example: newfs_msdos -F 16 /dev/disk3s1 Where /dev/disk3s1 is my SD card's name. Your card is now formatted.

Connecting the module to the Arduino

Connect the module to the Arduino, as shown in the following screenshot:

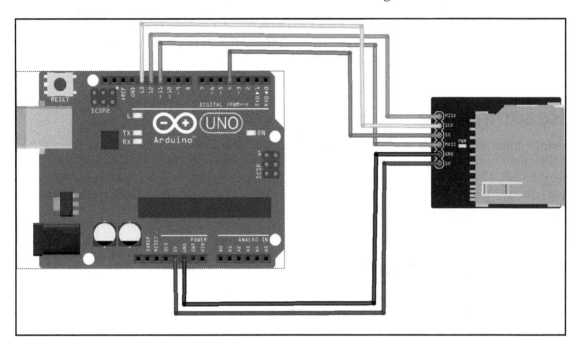

The preceding photo shows the following pin names:

Module pin	Arduino Uno Pin
5V	5V
GND	GND
MOSI	11
SS	4
SCK	13
MISO	12

You can use a Bread Board to simplify the connection with jumper wires.

Naming your data file

You must need a file to read or write on. You can either create one manually, on the PC, or create it using code. We will look at how we can create one using Arduino code. But, there is a limitation in the file naming of the FAT file system. The name must be of eight characters or fewer (for example, MYFILE.TXT, NAMEDATA.DOC, TimeFile.txt). The extension of the file must be of three characters (TXT, DOC, LOG, txt, doc, log, and so on).

Reading a file

Before going any further, we need to know a little bit about the Arduino library. A library is collection of code where a group of functions and operations are made and stored for further use. There are a number of libraries for Arduino. For file handling with the SD card, we have an Arduino library named SD.h library. We will discuss libraries in more detail in the following chapters.

Importing a library

To import a library to our Arduino project, click on Sketch and select Include Library. Look at the following screenshot to see how to select SD.h library for our project:

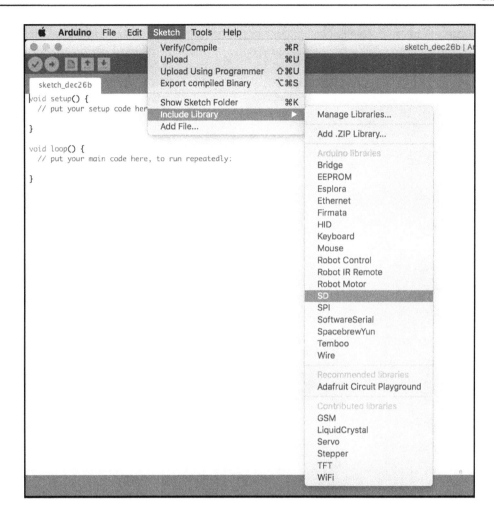

Setting CS/SS pin number

We have connected our CS/SS pin to our Arduino Uno's pin 4. This is important. Now, for Arduino, we need to select the output pin. The default pin for the output is 10. On Arduino Mega, the pin is 53. We can set the output pin as follows:

```
pinMode(10,OUTPUT);
```

Now it's time to check if our SD card is connected or not. We can do this by checking the SD.begin() function. Look at the following code to check if the card is initialized to the Arduino board or not:

```
if (!SD.begin(4)) {
   Serial.println("SD Card initialization failed :(");
}
else{
  Serial.println("SD Card initialization done :)");
   }
```

The full code to check if the SD card is connected or not is given below.

```
#include <SD.h>

void setup() {
  Serial.begin(9600);

  pinMode(10, OUTPUT);

  if (!SD.begin(4)) {
     Serial.println("SD Card initialization failed :(");
  }
  else{
    Serial.println("SD Card initialization done :)");
     }


}

void loop() {


}
```

Since the SD card is connected successfully, the output is as follows:

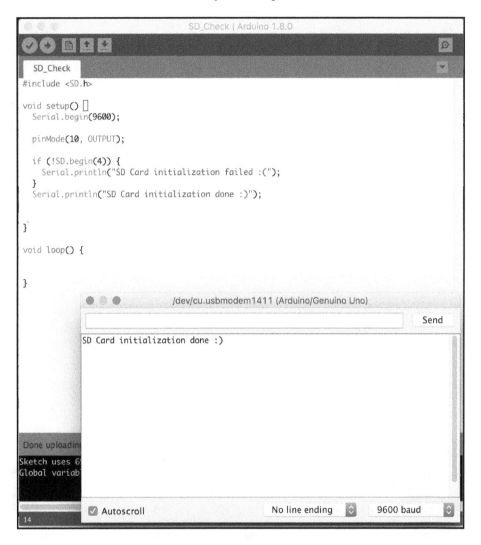

You may see the output as shown in the following screenshot:

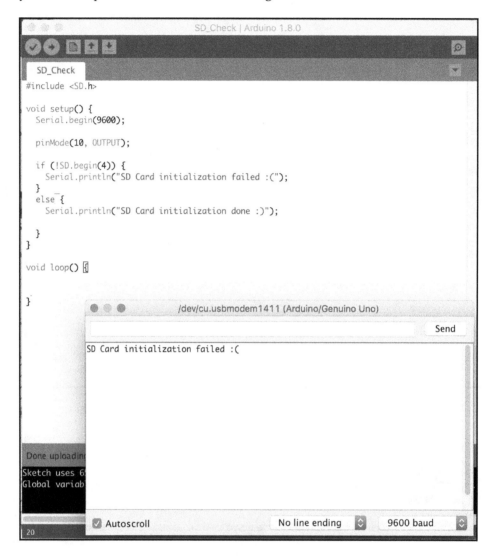

Don't worry if your output looks as shown in the preceding screenshot. Check the connection, port number, and code. If you have no luck, refer to `Chapter 10`, *Few Error Handlings*.

Now, create a text file on the SD card, which we will read from the Arduino:

1. Create the text file connecting the card directly to the computer. The text file may contain the following text, or any text you want:

   > Fear no more the heat o' the sun; Nor the furious winter's rages, Thou thy worldly task hast done, Home art gone, and ta'en thy wages; Golden lads and girls all must, As chimney sweepers come to dust.

2. Save the file as `poem.txt` format:

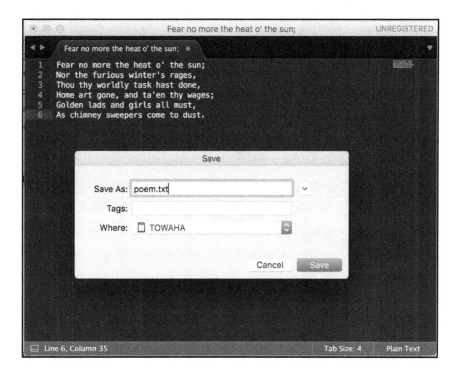

3. Now we will read the `poem.txt` file. To read the file, we need to use File Handling. To do this, we need to define a variable on top of our `setup()` function. Let's call our file `myFile`. So, declare the variable as follows:

```
File myFile;
```

4. After the initialization of the SD card, we need to open the file from the SD card. The function that opens files from the SD card is `SD.open()`. We will open the file and use our variable `myFile` as the file handle:

```
myFile = SD.open("poem.txt");
```

5. Inside the quotation marks, we need to write our file name. We sometimes need to write the directories too, if the file is inside some folders. If `SD.open()` can find the file on the SD card, we will read it by using a while loop and print the text using serial monitor . Then we will need to close the file. If we don't close the file, our file may get corrupted. So, the code for reading the file is as follows:

```
if (myFile) {
//Used to separate code
   Serial.println("===:The File Contains The following text:===");
  while (myFile.available()) { // Checking if the SD card has the file
     Serial.write(myFile.read()); // Reading file and printing on serial
    }
   myFile.close(); //closing the file
} else {
   Serial.println("error opening test.txt"); //If fine not available
}
```

6. Let's run our code and look at the output:

We have successfully read the file.

Writing on a file

Writing to a file using Arduino is similar to reading. For writing, we only need a few changes. We also need to open the file using `SD.open()`, but this time we need to pass two arguments into this function; the file name and the file opening mode. So, our `myFile` variable should be written as follows, after the card initialization is done. We will name our new file as `myFile.txt`:

```
myFile = SD.open("myFile.txt", FILE_WRITE);
```

Here, `FILE_WRITE` is the file mode. We need to pass this argument to open our file in writable mode. Now, if the file exists, we will print something using our File variable, which will be written on our myFile.txt file. After the writing is done, we will close the file to avoid any file corruption. Let's say we want to write the following lines on the `myFile.txt` file:

```
Twinkle, twinkle, little star How I wonder what you are
```

We need to print the lines as follows:

```
myFile.println("Twinkle, twinkle, little star ");
myFile.println("How I wonder what you are");

Let's see the full code.
#include <SD.h>
File myFile;
void setup() {
  Serial.begin(9600);
  pinMode(10, OUTPUT);
  if (!SD.begin(4)) {
    Serial.println("SD Card initialization failed :(");
  }
  else {
    Serial.println("SD Card initialization done :)");
  }
  myFile = SD.open("myFile.txt", FILE_WRITE);

  if (myFile) {
    Serial.println("==:Now we will write these lines on our file:==");
    Serial.println("Twinkle, twinkle, little star ");
    Serial.println("How I wonder what you are");
    myFile.println("Twinkle, twinkle, little star ");
    myFile.println("How I wonder what you are");
    Serial.println("Writing done. Closing the file........");
    myFile.close();
  } else {
```

```
        Serial.println("error opening file");
    }
}

void loop() {

}
```

Let's look at the output on the serial monitor:

Well, this is not proof our text is written on the file. Open the SD card from your PC, and let's explore if there is a file or not.

In my case, I opened the SD card and found a file named MYFILE.TXT. Inside the file, I found the text I wanted to write:

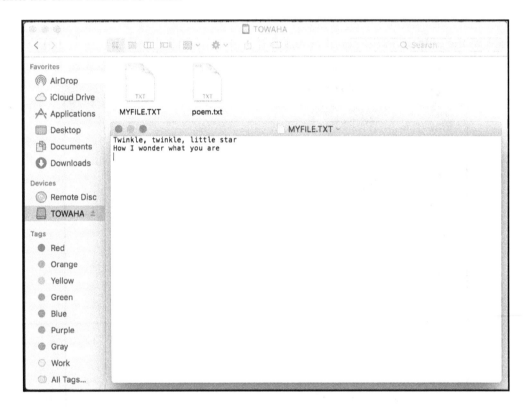

We can also read the file from our Arduino IDE with the following code. Can you tell where I made changes in the following code to read our text file?

```
#include <SD.h>
File myFile;
void setup() {
  Serial.begin(9600);

  pinMode(10, OUTPUT);

  if (!SD.begin(4)) {
    Serial.println("SD Card initialization failed :(");
  }
  else {
    Serial.println("SD Card initialization done :)");
  }

  myFile = SD.open("myfile.txt");
  if (myFile) {
    Serial.println("===:The File Contains The following text:===");
    while (myFile.available()) {
      Serial.write(myFile.read());
    }
    myFile.close();
  } else {
    Serial.println("error opening the file");
  }
}

void loop() {


}
```

The output file is as shown in the following screenshot:

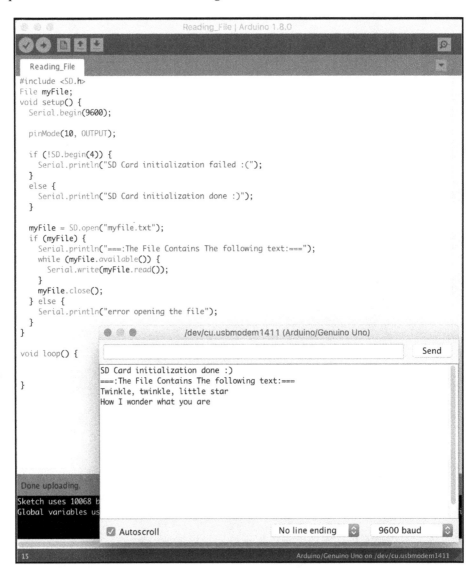

Exercise

1. Define two functions (named `sum()` and `sub()`) and pass two variables into them. Write the answers in a file, and after doing this, print the file content on serial monitor.

2. Read all data from a file and write it into another file.

3. Read four integers from a file and find the average of the number, showing the process on the serial monitor.

4. Suppose you have two files stored on an SD card. One file has five players' names and another file has their scores. Now make another file, containing both the names and scores side by side with the serial number. Look at the following screenshot for clarification:

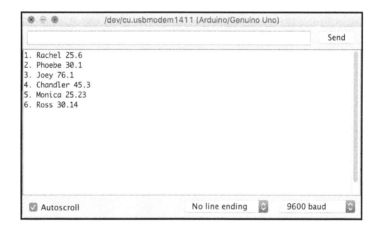

5. Write code to store all the integers inside a text file and find out the largest number. Then, the largest number will be both printed on the serial monitor and written on a separate file, with the following format, where `Number` is the largest number:

    +++++:::::::Number:::::::+++++

Summary

In this chapter, we have learned a number of important things for Arduino. We learned how to declare functions, how we can play with functions, how to connect an SD card to an Arduino, how to read a file from the SD card using Arduino Uno, and how to create a new file on the SD card with Arduino. We have also developed code for handling files with Arduino. There are a number of exercises in this chapter. These exercises are for broadening your thoughts about Arduino. What you can do with a small piece on computer. I hope you learn all the techniques in this chapter in order to gain a better understanding of Arduino programming. If you have enough knowledge about file handling, then I welcome you to the next chapter of this book: Chapter 6, *Arduino and C++*.

6
Arduino and C++

In this chapter, we are going to learn a lot of things. We will learn **Object Oriented Programming** (**OOP**), its characteristics, benefits, and using OOP with our Arduino programming. We will learn some keywords and uses of C++. We will also learn how to use a GSM module. We will use this module to make a call, send an SMS, and receive an SMS. So, let's get started.

Object Oriented Programming

Before talking about the more complex concepts within OOPs, we need to know what an Object Oriented Programming language is.

The C programming language is not an Object Oriented Programming language. In Arduino we use a modified version of C which can be compared to C++ programming. And, since C++ is an Object Oriented Programming language, we can implement the benefits of OOP in our Arduino projects.

An Object Oriented Programming language must have a few characteristics (inheritance, encapsulation, polymorphism, and so on) in order to be defined as an Object Oriented Programming language. C is an implementation language. In short, in C, we write a long code. But in OOPs, the code can be shortened using a number of techniques. These techniques are the OOPs's characters.

Objects

In our daily life, everything we see and feel is an object. The earth is an object, the moon is an object, a chair is an object-even your dog is an object. Whatever you can touch, smell, feel, or taste can be defined as an object.

In our real world, all objects have two characteristics: the state and the behavior.

The object `Dog` has states (`color`, `name`, `breed`, and so on) and behaviors (`barking`, `running`, `jumping`, `eating`, and so on). You can ask yourself what state an object has or what behavior an object may possess.

Your laptop is an object. Its states are switched on and switched off, and its behaviors are turning on and turning off.

There is another characteristic of objects, called **identity**. This is a unique reference marker for the object in question, they function in much the same way as a car's number plate. Each number plate is totally unique – one number plate cannot match with another.

We need to remember that an object is an instance of an abstract data type. If you don't know what an abstract data type is, don't worry – we will know it later.

We implement an abstract data type via a class. Let's learn a few things about class.

Class

In OOPs, there is another thing that is important to bear in mind while writing a code using OOP-class. Generally, a class is a blueprint of objects. It is a logical entity. But a class can be defined as the blueprint (a design plan) of an object or a group of objects. You may think of a class as a concept and an object as the embodiment of that concept.

So, Object Oriented programming is a technique to design our code or program using objects and classes.

Let's look at a few differences between Class and Object:

Object	Class
Object is anything we can touch or feel	Class is a description of the common properties of an object
Object is a part of data	Class is a part of a program
It is a phenomenon	It is a concept
Example type 1: John, Ron, Tom, Jim.	Example type 1: People
Example type 2: iPhone, Samsung, Alcatel, Nokia.	Example type 2: Mobile phone
Example type 3: Table, chair, couch, bed.	Example type 3: Furniture

Going deeper into class

When we declare a class, we need to start defining by class.

Class members can be of three types:

- Public
- Private
- Protected

Don't worry about these classifications for now. We will get into the types later.

Let's look at an example first.

A box has three dimensions-`length`, `width`, and `height`. We can define the `Box` class as follows:

```
class Box{
double lengthOfBox;
double heightOfBox;
double widthOfBox;
}
```

lengthOfBox, heightOfBox, and widthOfBox are the members of the Box class. If we want to make the class Public, Private, or Protected, we can declare them as follows:

```
class Box1 {
  Public:
    double lengthOfBox1;
    double heightOfBox1;
    double widthOfBox1;
};

class Box2 {
  Private:
    double lengthOfBox2;
    double heightOfBox2;
    double widthOfBox2;
};

class Box3 {
  Protected:
    double lengthOfBox3;
    double heightOfBox3;
    double widthOfBox3;
};
```

Let's make the Public, Private, and Protected types clear now:

- Box1 is a public class. We can call all the members of the public class from the main class and other classes.
- Box2 is a private class. We cannot call any members of the private class from the main class, but we can call them from the class itself.
- Box3 is a protected class. We cannot call any members of the protected class from the main class.

We can only access the private and protected classes from their own class. We will explain this later.

We can access any member of the aforementioned three classes by creating instances like the following:

```
Box1 obj1;
Obj1.lengthOfBox1;
Obj1.heightOfBox1;
Obj1.widthOfBox1;
```

Understanding OOP better

I know you've probably got a little bit of a headache if you are not familiar with the concept of OOP. Don't worry-keep reading and the idea of OOP will be clear to you soon. Let's start clarifying the situation by looking at an example involving functions.

Imagine a situation where you need to write the following print statements:

```
Serial.println("My name is John, I am 24 years old and my height 6.1
feet");
Serial.println("My name is Tom, I am 26 years old and my height 6.5 feet");
Serial.println("My name is Curl, I am 21 years old and my height 5.9
feet");
```

Have you noticed something in this code? The lines are almost similar. The only differences are the names, the age, and the height.

I know what you are thinking: We can make a function with three parameters like the following:

```
void myFunction(String name, int age, float height) {
  Serial.println("My name is ");
  Serial.print(name);
  Serial.print(", I am ");
  Serial.print(age);
  Serial.print(" years old and my height is ");
  Serial.print(height);
  Serial.print(" feet");
}
```

Just a short note-in OOP, instead of using the `term` function, we use the `term` method. Let's compare the output of each code first. The code with the function will be executed with the following parameters:

```
myFunction("John", 24, 6.1);
myFunction("Tom", 26, 6.5);
myFunction("Curl", 21, 5.9);
```

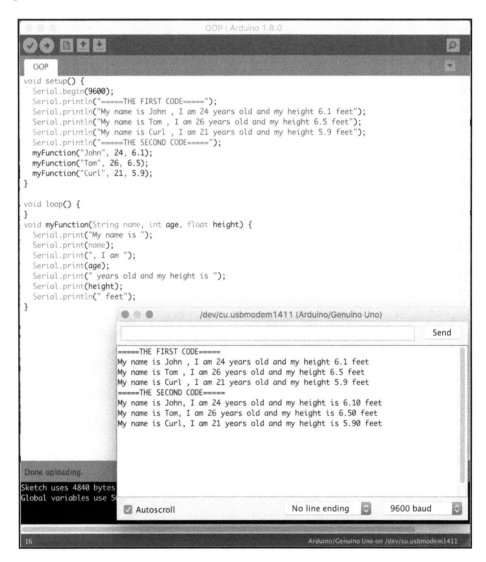

From the output, you can see that both programs give the same answers. The second one is more efficient than the first one because we can call our function with only three parameters any time without writing the entire line of code.

Now we have a problem for the second type of code. We do not know which value is John's age, or which value is Tom's height; we just passed our parameters into the myFunction(). But we could make the program more efficient by making a class. Let's do this. This time we will make three types of class:

```
class john {
  public:
    String name = "John";
    int age = 24;
    float height = 6.1;
};
class tom {
  private:
    String name = "Tom";
    int age = 26;
    float height = 6.5;
};
class curl {
  protected:
    String name = "Curl";
    int age = 21;
    float height = 5.9;
};
```

Note that we need to put a semicolon after each of the classes in C for Arduino. After the type of class (public, private, and so on) we must add a colon (:) symbol.

Now let's try to get the values from the john class. We need to make a type for the class first:

```
john myObj;
```

Now we can access any members of the class `john`:

```
myObj.name; //This is equal to John
myObj.age; // This is equal to 24
myObj.height;//This is equal to 6.1
```

We can use them either by storing with another variable or directly.

We can now print the variables as per usual:

```
Serial.print("My name is ");
Serial.print(myObj.name);
Serial.print(", I am ");
Serial.print(myObj.age);
Serial.print(" years old and my height is ");
Serial.print(myObj.height);
```

Let's see the output and the full code:

```
class john {
  public:
    String name = "John";
    int age = 24;
    float height = 6.1;
};

void setup() {
  Serial.begin(9600);
  john myObj;
  Serial.print("My name is ");
  Serial.print(myObj.name);
  Serial.print(", I am ");
  Serial.print(myObj.age);
  Serial.print(" years old and my height is ");
  Serial.print(myObj.height);
}

void loop() {

}
```

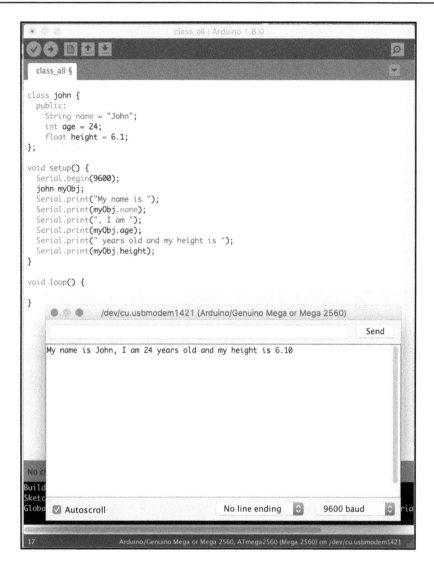

Our class is still not perfect. Let's make a function inside our `john`class:

```
class john {
  public:
    String name = "John";
    int age = 24;
    float height = 6.1;
    void JohnInfo() {
      Serial.print("My name is ");
      Serial.print(this->name);
```

```
        Serial.print(", I am ");
        Serial.print(this->age);
        Serial.print(" years old and my height is ");
        Serial.print(this->height);
      }
  };
```

We used the `->`symbol to access the members of a class inside the class itself. Let's call the function from the `setup()` function and see the output. The whole code will look like the following:

```
class john {
  public:
    String name = "John";
    int age = 24;
    float height = 6.1;
    void JohnInfo() {
      Serial.print("My name is ");
      Serial.print(this->name);
      Serial.print(", I am ");
      Serial.print(this->age);
      Serial.print(" years old and my height is ");
      Serial.print(this->height);
    }
};

void setup() {
  Serial.begin(9600);
  john myObj;
  myObj.JohnInfo();
}

void loop() {

}
```

This class is now complete for John, but what about the other two people? Why don't we make the class more efficient for everybody? Let's rename the class to `peopleInfo` and add arguments to the class's function as follows so that our class can be a reusable blueprint:

```
class PeopleInfo {
  private:
    String name;
    int age;
    float height;
  public:
    void getInfo(String PeopleName, int PeopleAge, float PeopleHeight) {
      name = PeopleName;
      age = PeopleAge;
      height = PeopleHeight;
      Serial.print("My name is ");
      Serial.print(name);
```

```
Serial.print(", I am ");
Serial.print(age);
Serial.print(" years old and my height is ");
Serial.print(height);

}

};
```

The entity name, age, and height are kept inside the private part and the function is kept in the public part. We called the private variables from the public part. It is possible because we called them from the same class. If we call the properties of the private part from our main class, we will get an error. Let's test it. Inside our `setup()` function, let's call the variables of the private part:

Yes, we got an error. The error says, **String PeopleInfo::name' is private String name**. Now let's call the function which is not private, and look at the result:

Yes, it worked! Can you write the code to show other people's information? I bet you can.

Let's look at a few more things about OOPs.

Fundamentals of OOP

An OOPs Language has a few essential characteristics. Without these characteristics, we cannot call a programming language an OOPs language. These characteristics are also called the principles of Objective Oriented Programming. The characteristics are as follows:

- Encapsulation
- Data Abstraction
- Polymorphism
- Inheritance

Let's look at the characteristics in detail.

Encapsulation

Encapsulation is an information hiding mechanism. It combines both code and data together. Encapsulation is used to hide the values of an object inside a class. It prevents an unauthorized section of code from accessing the code directly. Before discussing encapsulation any further, let's look at a simple example. Look at the following code:

```
class AddNumbers {
  public:
    int addNumbersFunction(void) {
      return num1 + num2;
    }

  private:
    int num1 = 4;
    int num2 = 5 ;
};
```

The `AddNumbers` class has two sections-`public` and `private`.

The public section has a function called `addNumbersFunction`, which returns the sum of two integer variables-`num1` and `num2`. The `num1` and `num2` variables are under the private section. It means they can only be accessed from the `AddNumbers` class. They cannot be accessed from any other part of the program. This is simply an encapsulation of the data. The output of the program will definitely return the sum of 4 and 5, which is 9.

Let's see if we can get the output from our `setup()` class. Our code for the `setup()` function will be as follows:

```
void setup() {
  Serial.begin(9600);
  AddNumbers getSum;
  int mySum = getSum.addNumbersFunction(); //Stored the return value
  Serial.print("The sum is ");
  Serial.print(mySum);

}
```

The code inside the `setup()` function, we stored the return value of the public function `addNumbersFunction()` to an integer `mySum`. We can directly print by using the following method:

```
void setup() {
  Serial.begin(9600);
  AddNumbers getSum;
  Serial.print("The sum is ");
  Serial.print(getSum.addNumbersFunction()); // directly printed.
}
```

From the output, we can see that the sum is correct. Let's see if we can call the variables outside the `AddNumbers` class. We can do this by writing the following code:

```
void setup() {
  Serial.begin(9600);
  AddNumbers getSum;
  int n1 = getSum.num1; // Storing to an integer
  int n2 = getSum.num2;
  Serial.print("The sum is ");
  Serial.print(n1 + n2); //Printed the sum
}
```

Now, let's see the output:

Now we see an error! So, what does the error say? It says, **'int AddNumbers::num1' is private**.

So, finally we can say that we cannot call the private variables outside the class itself. Let's look at a few more things about encapsulation in brief:

- Encapsulation combines the state and behavior
- It secures data from other methods
- It protects an object from unauthorized access by clients
- It provides pure abstraction between an object and its clients

Data Abstraction

Data Abstraction is kind of similar to encapsulation, but it has two functions:

- Providing information to the other part of the program
- Hiding the background details

Let's look at an example. Your smartphone can do lot of things. It can make calls, connect to the Internet, send text messages, and so on. We can add an earphone, charger, and other extensions to it. But we do not know what is happening inside the smartphone – how it transmits the signals, how it processes data inside its processors, how the graphics are handled. We sometimes do not need to know the background process of a task. For such cases we use Data Abstraction. Before getting to the programming part, we need to know what a Constructor is.

Constructor

Constructor is like a member function or method that initializes an instance of the class. The constructor must have the same name as the class. A constructor does not have any return value. A constructor may have any number of arguments. The constructor may have any kind of accessibility depending on how we declare it. We can declare a constructor as private, public, or protected. If we do not declare the constructor, the compiler will generate a default constructor. The default constructor does not have any parameter. Look at the following code of a constructor:

```
class ArduinoClass {

   public:
      ArduinoClass(int numOFClass, String stdName, bool present) {


      }
};
The default constructor may look like the following:
```

```
class ArduinoClass {

    ArduinoClass() {

    }
}
```

Now let's look at writing code for Data Abstraction. Any Arduino program where we can implement a class with public and private members is an example of Data Abstraction.

Let's do something meaningful. Say you have a bank account and you save money into this account every month or week. You want to track your savings. You can write a program for this, but you do not want to let other people know the total amount by accessing the public class's members.

To do this, let's first write our class with a constructor. Our constructor will be `public`. The class will be as follows:

```
class Account {
  public:
    // constructor of the Account class
    Account(int i = 0) {
    }
```

We have a parameter for the constructor (`int i = 0`) which will be used to store the total amount of money we save on our account. Let's write two interfaces inside the class with public access. The interfaces will be named `addMoney` and `getTotalAmount`. Our `addMoney` interface will look like as follows:

```
    void addMoney(int number) {
    }
```

We have an integer type parameter (`number`) that passes to the `addMoney` interface. This will store the temporary amount we want to store on our account. The `getTotalAmount` interface looks as follows:

```
    int getTotalAmount() {
    }
```

The `getTotalAmount` interface does not have any arguments. It will return the total amount we will save on our account. Now, let's come to the secret part of our code. We want to hide the total amount from the other class, so we will make it private as follows:

```
  private:
    // Total will be hidden from other classes
    int total;
```

We need to increment the value of the total each time we add money to our account, so our addMoney interface should look like the following:

```
void addMoney(int number) {
     total += number; //incrementing value
   }
```

So, our total Account class should look like the following:

```
class Account {
  public:
    Account(int i = 0) {
      total = i; //assigned total to integer i.
    }
    void addMoney(int number) {
      total += number;
    }
    int getTotalAmount() {
      return total;
    }

  private:
    int total;
};
```

It's time to write our main code. Our setup class should be like the following:

```
void setup() {
  Serial.begin(9600);
  Account bank; // Do you know what does it mean?
  bank.addMoney(5000); // Our first deposit
  bank.addMoney(1100); // Our second deposit
  bank.addMoney(6000); // Our third deposit
}
```

If we want to see how much we saved, we can print bank.getTotalAmount(). Because this returns total, we cannot directly call total from our setup function or any function other than the Account class. This is how our account is secured by using Data Abstraction.

Let's look at the output of our code. It should return **12100**, right?

Yes! Our code is perfect.

Virtual function

Remember, an `abstract` class must have a `virtual` function. A `virtual` function is a method that must be overridden by its derived classes. Look at the following code of the `virtual` function of an `abstract` class:

```
class abstract {
    virtual int myFunction() = 0;
};
```

We define the virtual function with the keyword virtual and set the function as equal to zero.

Polymorphism

We will now look at another interesting characteristic of OOPs-polymorphism. Polymorphism is a Greek word. It means many forms. In OOP, polymorphism allows an interface to be used for a general class of actions. It is the ability of a class to take on multiple forms. Polymorphism occurs when there is a number of classes that are related so that they can reach others. Polymorphism also means that some operations or objects behave differently in different contexts. In C++, we have an operator called plus (+). Using the plus operator, we can do a number of things. Such as the following:

- 8 + 7.8 – Floating point addition
- 12 + 8 – Integer addition
- String1 + another string-String concatenation (adding two strings together)

I suppose that by now you are kind of bored with the theory. Let's look at a real-life scenario. Say you want to build a game. In your game, you have a hero who has different kinds of enemies-dragon, evil man, ninja, dinosaur, and so on. Though all the enemies are different, they have one thing in common: They all need to attack the hero. Their style of attacking is also different. The attack function can work on all different types of objects. What the polymorphism characteristic basically allows you to do is use the same method and have many different outcomes.

Before writing any code using polymorphism, we need to learn the terms pointer and reference. The use of pointers and references will be discussed in more detail on `Chapter 7`, *Using Pointers and Structure*. In this chapter, however, we will get a general idea about using pointers and references.

Pointer and reference in polymorphism

A pointer is kind of similar to the other variables. It can store data, but unlike other variables (integers, floats, string, and so on) a pointer stores a memory address.

I will make it easy for you a little bit later. For now, let us look at how we can declare a pointer.

The pointer can be of any type. It can be an integer, it can be a character, and so on. The main thing you should remember while declaring a pointer is that you need to put an asterisk (*) before the name of the pointer. Look at the following example:

```
int *myVar;
char *time;
double *number;
```

The asterisk (*) can be placed anywhere in between the type of the variable and the name of the variable:

```
int *num;
int* num;
int * num;
```

These all are correct.

Assume we declared a variable as follows:

```
int num = 90;
```

You can clearly say the value of num is 90. This 90 is stored somewhere on our Arduino microcontroller, right? Let's find out the memory address of the integer where it is saved. We need to declare a pointer first:

```
int *pNum;
Here *pNum is our pointer.
```

That's all we need to know about pointers for now. Let's move on to two important topics for learning **polymorphism** - **method overloading** and **method overriding** - and then we will finish by looking at a basic example.

Method overload

In C++, we can define multiple types of functions (based on their return types and parameters) with the same name in the same scope. This mechanism is known as function overloading or method overloading. This is also called static polymorphism.

Let's look at an example.

We will create a class called *operation*. Inside *operation*, we will define few methods with the same name.

We will declare four methods inside our `operation` class:

```
void demo() {
  }
void demo(int x) {
}
void demo(int x, int y) {
}
void demo(double x, double y) {
}
```

The first method does not have any parameter. The other three methods have different numbers and types of parameters.

Our program will automatically know when we called our method with parameters without parameters, or even with different types of parameters.

Let's call them from our `setup()` function.

We first need to create an object of the operation class to access the members and method of the class. Then we will use the temporary object and call the methods:

```
operation obj; //Created temporary object
obj.demo();    //called the 1st method
obj.demo(2);   // Called the 2nd method
obj.demo(3, 4); //called the 3rd method
obj.demo(3.1, 8.9); // called the 4th method.
```

The full code will look like the following:

```
class operation {

  public:
    void demo() {
      Serial.println("No Parameter");
    }
    void demo(int x) {
      Serial.print("One Parameter which is x = ");
      Serial.println(x);
    }
    void demo(int x, int y) {
      Serial.print("Two Parameters they are x = ");
      Serial.print(x);
      Serial.print(" and y = ");
      Serial.println(y);
    }
    void demo(double x, double y) {
      Serial.print("Double parameters;  x = ");
      Serial.print(x);
      Serial.print(" and y = ");
      Serial.println(y);
    }
};

void setup() {
  Serial.begin(9600);
  operation obj;
  obj.demo();
  obj.demo(2);
  obj.demo(3, 4);
  obj.demo(3.1, 8.9);
}
void loop() {


}
```

Now we will look at the output and see if our program has correctly overloaded the methods:

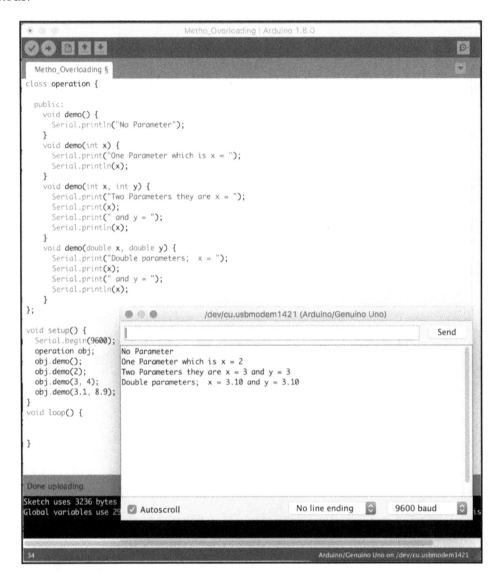

Yes, the output is perfect! The methods are successfully overloaded. Let's look at another term called method override.

Method overriding

Method overriding refers to a subclass or child class that has the same method or function as the parent class. Or we can say, if a subclass provides the specific implementation of the method that is similar to the parent class's method, then then this is an instance of a method override. This is also called dynamic polymorphism.

Suppose we have a class called `baseClass`, as follows:

```
class baseClass {
  public:
    void methodOverride() {
      Serial.println("Base");
    }
};
Now we will extend the class by the extendClass class:
class extendClass : public baseClass {
  public:
    void methodOverride() {
      Serial.println("Extend");
    }
};
```

Inside the `setup()` function, we will now create the base class's pointer and extended class's object. So now, our final code of the `setup()` function will be like the following code:

```
void setup() {
  Serial.begin(9600);
  baseClass* b;         //Base class pointer
  extendClass d;        //Extended class object
  b = &d;
  b->methodOverride();
}
```

What do you think? The object is of the `extendClass`, so the object class method should be called, right? No, you are wrong. For method overriding and early binding, the base class's method will be called.

Let's look at the output of the code:

Now let's go back to our main topic – polymorphism. Did I mention that polymorphism has two types? They are runtime polymorphism and other is compile-time polymorphism. Compile-time polymorphism is nothing but the two examples we just learned (method overloading and method overriding). Runtime polymorphism needs a virtual function.

Runtime polymorphism is a form of polymorphism where function binding occurs when the program runs.

We can have parameters in our subclass with the same name as the base class. A virtual keyword is used in the base class to call the subclass. The method call only takes place during the runtime.

Let's look at a simple example of run time polymorphism:

```
class Food {
  public:
    virtual void eat() {
      Serial.println("This is the Food class");
    }
};

class Chocolate: public Food {
  public:
    void eat() {

      Serial.println("This is a chocolate class");
    }
};


void setup() {
  Serial.begin(9600);
  Food * fd;
  Chocolate ch;
  fd = &ch;
  fd->eat();
}

void loop() {
  // put your main code here, to run repeatedly:

}
```

The preceding code has two class - Food and Chocolate. The class Chocolate is the subclass of the Food class. We can also call the Chocolate class as the child class of the Food class. In the Food class, we used the virtual keyword that indicates the member method (eat()) of the Chocolate class. In the setup() function, we called the member class by using the pointer of the Food class.

Our program should show **This is a chocolate class** in the serial monitor. Let's look at the output of the code:

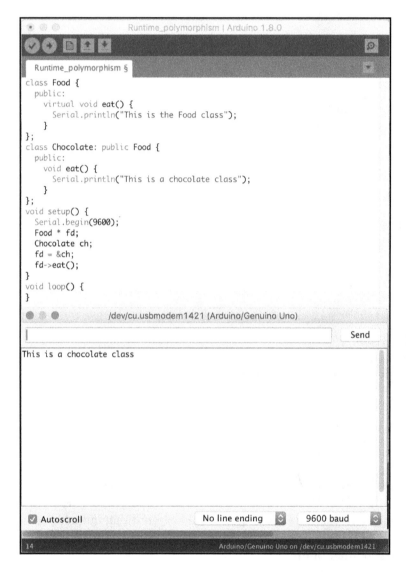

Yes, our code runs correctly. Let's look at another characteristic of OOP – Inheritance.

Inheritance

Inherit means *derive a quality, characteristic, or predisposition genetically from one's parents or ancestors.* In OOPs, inheritance means inheriting the data and members of the previous class or the base class to another class. Let's make it clear: Inheritance allows the creation of hierarchical classifications. Using inheritance, we can define a class in terms of another class. While creating a new class, instead of writing new members and their objects, we can define that the new class should inherit the members of an existing class. The existing class can be defined as the base class and the new class will be called the extended or the derived class.

Let's write a base class named `Person`. We will create three sub-classes named Teacher, Student, and Programmer.

All the characters are persons. They can talk, they can run, they can walk, they can eat. But some have special kinds of skills.

A teacher teaches, a student learns, and a programmer writes code. So, the person class should look like the following:

```
class Person {
public:
String Profession;
void SerialPrint() {
Serial.print("I am a ");
Serial.println(Profession);
walk();
eat();
talk();
}
void walk() {
Serial.println("I can walk");
}
void eat() {
Serial.println("I can eat");
}
void talk() {
Serial.println("I can talk");
}
};
```

We have created four methods inside our person class. The `SerialPrint()` method will display the output on the Serial Monitor. This is common for all the people. Let's write the three child classes extending the person class:

```cpp
class Teacher : public Person {
public:
void teach() {
Serial.println("I teach!");
}
};
class Student : public Person {
public:
void study() {
Serial.println("I study!");
}
};
class Programmer : public Person {
public:
void code() {
Serial.println("I code!");
}
};
```

Each of the subclasses has a unique method, but all of them inherited the methods and members of the person class. Let's test it by invoking the person and its child classes.

To print the characteristics of the teacher, we need to write the following code inside out `setup()` function:

```cpp
Teacher teacher; //Created an object
teacher.Profession = "Teacher"; //Assigned to the String Profession
teacher.SerialPrint(); //Called common characteristics
teacher.teach(); //called unique character
```

Can you code for the other two persons? I bet you can. The full code is given here in case you need help:

```cpp
class Person {

public:
  String Profession;
  void SerialPrint() {
    Serial.print("I am a ");
    Serial.println(Profession);
    walk();
    eat();
    talk();
```

```
      }
      void walk() {
        Serial.println("I can walk");
      }
      void eat() {
        Serial.println("I can eat");
      }
      void talk() {
        Serial.println("I can talk");
      }
};
class Teacher : public Person {
  public:
      void teach() {
        Serial.println("I teach!");
      }
};
class Student : public Person {
  public:
      void study() {
        Serial.println("I study!");
      }
};
class Programmer : public Person {
  public:
      void code() {
        Serial.println("I code!");
      }
};
void setup() {
  Serial.begin(9600);
  Teacher teacher;
  teacher.Profession = "Teacher";
  teacher.SerialPrint();
  teacher.teach();
  Student student;
  student.Profession = "Student";
  student.SerialPrint();
  student.study();
  Programmer programmer;
  programmer.Profession = "Programmer";
  programmer.SerialPrint();
  programmer.code();
}
void loop() {
}
```

Let's look at the output of the code:

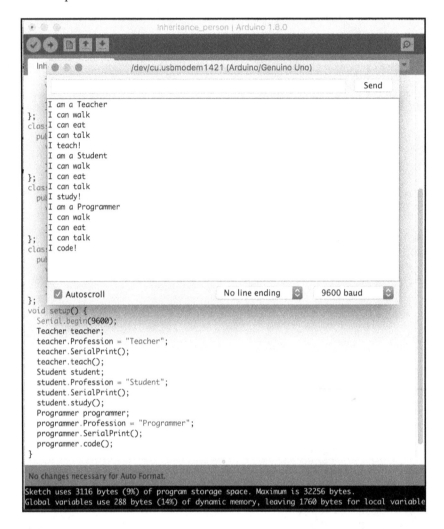

I hope the Object Oriented Program's characteristics are clear to you.

Let's go through the following exercises using the basic OOP characteristics.

Exercises

- Write a program with a parent class and an inherited child class. Both of them should have a common method `PrintScreen()` that prints the messages of both classes when invoked from the `setup()` function. (Hint: Create an object of the classes and call the function.)
- Using an OOP concept, write a program that will show the area of a triangle, a circle, and a rectangle. (Hints: Make a class with a constructor and three `getArea()` methods for the three shapes. Use the polymorphism characteristic for passing different number of parameters. You already know how you can find the area of the shapes from your math class, right?)
- Using method overriding, write a program with a base class and its extended class. From the `setup()` function, make the program to print all the statements of the base class while the extended class is invoked.

Benefits of OOP

OOPs has a great advantage over other programming styles. OOP is not related to programming; it is just a concept. Let's look at a few of the benefits of the OOPs:

- **Reusing the same code**: OOPs helps us code less. We need to code fewer lines than other languages that do not support OOPs concepts. We can reuse the same code for different classes and call any method when needed.
- **Security of the program**: OOPs helps programmers to build secure software and keep vulnerable code hidden from hackers and other unauthorized access.
- **Tidiness of the code**: After the invention of the OOP concept, code could become more beautiful and easy to understand. Now, because of OOP, we write less code and make our entire program neat and clean.
- **Upgrading existing software**: Because of OOPs, any system running using OOPs-driven programs can be updated easily.
- **Complexity of software**: OOP reduces the complexity of our programs, and so we now create software with less bugs.
- **Reducing redundancy**: By using OOP, we solve the problem of data redundancy. We use inheritance to reduce the redundancy in our program.

- **Good framework**: OOPs provides a number of good frameworks for coding libraries where supplied software components can be easily adapted and modified.
- **Easy Refactoring**: Using the OOP concept, we can refactor our program easily. We do not need to change many lines of code if we want to refactor the code.

Using OOP with Arduino

In Arduino, we can write our programs by inline coding and by using OOP concepts. The question is, why should we use the OOP concepts in our code while writing programs with Arduino? Remember from the first chapter that Arduino is a small computer with little memory. The larger our code, the larger the amount of memory that will be occupied by Arduino. So, our first intention should be saving the memory wastage, and OOP is the best solution. Using abstract classes, virtual methods, and other OOP concepts in our Arduino programming, we can write our code without wasting a large amount of the tiny memory of the VRAM of our Arduino. Since we can reuse our code and inherit methods, we can make our program tiny using the OOP methodology. We will discuss OOP in Arduino further in the forthcoming chapters. In this chapter, we will use OOP to shorten our code. Before you start the next topic, I would recommend that you collect the necessary devices and boards for your Arduino.

GSM modules

GSM stands for **Global System for Mobile** communication. It was introduced in 1991. Using GSM and other technology, we can make phone calls, send **SMS (Short Message Service)**, and connect to the Internet. About 82.4% of the global mobile communication is represented by GSM. In this section of the chapter, we will learn how to choose a perfect GSM module for our Arduino, connect it to the Arduino, make a call using the GSM module, and send SMS. So, let's get started.

Types of GSM module

There are three types of GSM (not GSM modules), each with a different frequency. They are GSM, EGSM, and DCS. We will stick to GSM in this section. For Arduino we will use a GSM shield. There are a number of GSM shields in the market. Look at the following images:

This shield can be used with almost any Arduino:

This shield can be used with any Arduino board:

This board requires an Arduino Uno and 5V external power:

This board requires an Arduino Mega and 5V external power.

Before buying any GSM module, you need to know which GSM shield is perfect for you and for your country. GSM modules differ from country to country because of the frequencies allowed by the country.

The top GSM shield models are SIM900, SIM900A, SIM900A mini, and so on. In this chapter, we will use SIM900A Mini. The following image is a SIM900A Mini GSM shield:

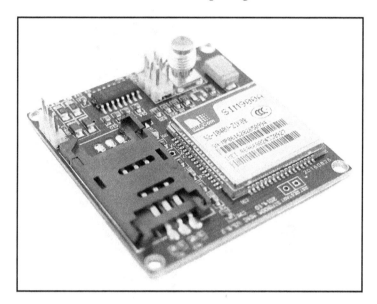

Getting to know SIM900A mini better

Your SIM900A Mini will come with an antenna. First of all, connect the antenna to the golden jack. Place the antenna bottom on the top of the jack and rotate it clockwise until you get a firm bonding between the board and the antenna. There are nine pins on the SIM900A Mini.

Look at the following image to see the names of the pins:

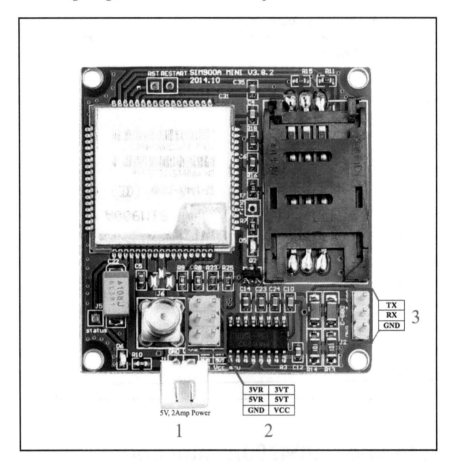

1. The module has two pins for external power. We can use a 5V, 2amp external power supply to power up the shield, or we can use the Arduino pins to power up the GSM shield. It is highly recommended that you use an external power supply because the Arduino might not be able to supply enough power to the shield. The maximum power can vary depending on the model of the board.
2. These six pins are for installing jumpers. This group of pins is called the **RS232** port. This port can be used to connect our computer directly via the serial connector. These pins will not be used for coding in this chapter.
3. These three pins are the most important pins for this chapter. The pins are **TX**, **RX** and **GND**.

4. **TX**, **RX** and **GND** are the abbreviations for **Transmit**, **Receive** and **Ground** respectively. You may be wondering what the *X* refers to in TX and RX. Well, it does not mean anything at all. *X* is used with TX and RX to make the acronyms more acceptable.

Connecting the GSM Shield to the Arduino

Before connecting the GSM Shield to our Arduino, let's look at what the pins of the GSM Shield do.

The TX and RX pins do a number of things. To simplify their tasks, we can say the pins are used to communicate between the Arduino and the computer.

We will not be using the port RS232, so let's skip this port. The power port usually needs a power maximum of 5V and 2Amp. We will have to use an external power supply for this.

To prepare our GSM Shield for use, we first need to insert a SIM card into the port. Make sure the SIM card fits in the port and lock the port. Look at the following image for inserting the SIM and locking the port:

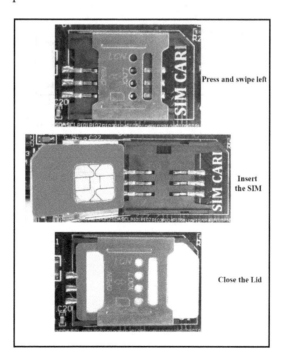

Now, we will use jumper wires (female to male jumper wire) to connect the TX and RX pins to the Arduino board.

In our case, connect the TX pin to the Arduino pin 2 and RX pin to the Arduino pin 3.

The ground pin should be connected to the Arduino GND pin. We can connect the GSM power pins to the Arduino pins. The 5V pin of the GSM Shield should be connected to the Arduino 5V pin and the ground (GND) pin should be connected to the Arduino ground pin. Look at the following diagram for clarification. I do not recommend that you use the Arduino board to power up the GSM Shield, but we can use this GSM Shield with the Arduino board:

Now connect your Arduino to the PC and make sure the onboard LEDs of the Arduino light up.

The onboard LEDs of the GSM Shield should also light up. If you are not sure about the position of the LED of the GSM Shield, Look at the following image:

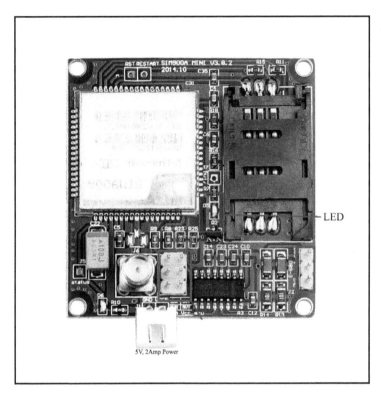

The LED of the GSM Shield will blink randomly if it does not receive the mobile network. When the SIM card is successfully configured to the GSM Shield, the LED on the GSM Shield will stop blinking randomly and will start to blink once per second.

Now that we have successfully connected our Arduino and the GSM Shield, let's move on to the coding part.

Before coding for the GSM Shield, we need to know a little bit about the Arduino library.

In Chapter 8, *Working with Arduino Libraries*, we will learn about the Arduino libraries in detail. For this section, we only need to know what the library is and why we need to use it.

Arduino library

We already used a `SD.h` library in our previous chapter. By the term **library**, we usually mean collection of books or files. It can be a collection of anything. In programming, a library can be defined as the routines of precompiled code and programs. The routine may contain a number of necessary methods, classes, and other definitions. In a nutshell, a library is a collection of code written previously to be used when necessary. When you installed the Arduino IDE, a number of famous Arduino libraries had been installed to the Arduino directory. You can find them in the library folder. In my case, I found the following libraries installed when I installed Arduino IDE on my machine:

- `Adafruit_CircuitPlayground`
- `Bridge`
- `Esplora`
- `Ethernet`
- `Firmata`
- `GSM`
- `Keyboard`
- `LiquidCrystal`
- `Mouse`
- `Robot_Control`
- `Robot_Motor`
- `RobotIRremote`
- `SD`
- `Servo`
- `SpacebrewYun`
- `Stepper`
- `Temboo`
- `TFT`
- `WiFi`

In the `Chapter 8`, *Working with Arduino Libraries*, we will learn about a few famous libraries and their usages. In using our GSM Shield, we will need the GSM library. We can also use the `SoftwareSerial` library if we want to avoid making errors in the code.

Since this chapter is not about libraries, we will use the `SotwareSerial` library to avoid needless complexity. You should be able to use any library after we finish `Chapter 8`, *Working with Arduino Libraries*.

Making a call using GSM module

Your Arduino and the GSM Shield are connected and powered up. First, open the Arduino IDE and import the `SoftwareSerial.h` library, as shown in the previous chapter, or go to the menu shown in the following image (**Sketch** | **IncludeLibrary** | **SoftwareSerial**):

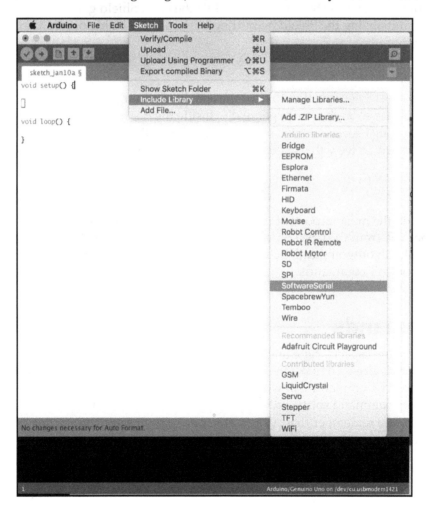

You can also manually type the following line on the top of the `setup()` function:

```
#include <SoftwareSerial.h>
```

Now, we will define the pins of the Arduino where TX and RX will be attached as follows:

```
SoftwareSerial GSMSerial(2, 3); //Pin 2 is our TX and 3 is the RX
```

Here, `GSMSerial()` is a custom function which will be used later. You can name it anything you want. We passed two parameters into this function. The first parameter is for the TX pin and the second parameter is for the RX pin.

Let's print something on the Serial Monitor while the GSM Shield get ready to work. Then we will begin initializing the Shield by putting the baud rate inside our `GSMSerial()` object, as follows:

```
GSMSerial.begin(9600);
```

We will use the `delay()` function to hold the activities of our program for a moment so that the GSM Shield has enough time to get ready. Inside the `delay()` function, we use time in a millisecond format (1 second = 1000 milliseconds). We will wait 1 second for the GSM Shield to get ready, so we will use the following code under the `GSMSerial()` object:

```
GSMSerial.begin(9600).
delay(1000);
```

Now we will do the most important part of our coding. We will use an AT command to make a phone call from the GSM Shield's SIM card. Make sure the SIM card has enough balance to make an outgoing call. Before writing the code for calling, we need to know a few things about AT commands.

AT commands

AT Commands are a special type of command for communicating with the GSM or other communication devices. To make the list of devices shorter, we would call the devices as modems, so an AT Command will work on the control of a modem. AT is the short form of attention. Every command starts with `AT` or `at`-that's why we call these commands `AT` Commands. Please remember that AT is a prefix only, represents the starting of an `AT` Command. This is not a part of the `AT` Command itself.

The syntax of an `AT` Command is *AT+COMMAND*.

Usages and rules of AT Commands

There are a number of important uses and rules of AT Commands. A few of them are as follows:

- Sending and receiving a text
- Getting basic information about the GSM Shield
- Establishing a data connection
- Performing security-related tasks
- Getting the current state of the GSM Shield
- Getting or changing the configuration of mobile phones.
- Read, write, or delete phonebook contact information saved on the SIM card.
- The basic AT commands do not start with a plus (+) sign. To call using a GSM we use D, to answer a call we use A. We will discuss the commands later.
- For SMS sending and receiving, we use AT+CMGS command followed by other code. We will also learn them later.

For calling a phone number, we need to send an AT command to the Arduino, and the Arduino will send it to the GSM Shield. We will pass our AT Commands by the following method:

```
GSMSerial.println("Our AT Commands;");
```

Inside the quotation, we will write our AT Commands. You must use a semicolon (;) after each of the AT Commands. To call a number using an AT Command, our AT Command will be ATD##############; (D is used here because we are going to dial a number from the GSM Shield and call the desired number.) The ############## is the phone number that we want to call. It is a good practice to use the phone number with the country code (without the + sign). To make sure we have successfully sent the AT Command to the GSM board, we will print something on the Serial Monitor after the GSMSerial.println(); is called. So the code will be like the following:

```
GSMSerial.println("ATD#############;");
Serial.println("Calling ATD#############");
```

Now let's see the full source code for calling from the GSM Shield:

```
#include <SoftwareSerial.h>
SoftwareSerial GSMSerial(2, 3);
void setup() {
  Serial.begin(9600); //Setting the Arduino Baud rate
  Serial.println("Warming Up the GSM Shield; Look at the Shield's LED");
  Serial.println("..........");
```

```
    Serial.println(".............");
    Serial.println("..................");
    Serial.println(".......................");
    GSMSerial.begin(9600); //Setting GSM's Baud rate
    delay(1000); //Waiting 1 sec for GSM to work.
    GSMSerial.println("ATD#############;"); // Calling a number
    Serial.println("Calling ATD#############");
    Serial.println(".........");
    Serial.println(".............");
    Serial.println("..................");
    Serial.println(".......................");
}

void loop() {

}
```

Let's see if our code runs properly, and whether we receive a call from the Arduino.

The output of the code on the serial monitor is as follows:

I called my phone number, and yes, I did indeed get a call from my Arduino! Look at the screenshot from my phone:

Isn't it exciting? You may be wondering how you can really use your GSM Shield to talk over the phone. Well, you will need a microphone and a speaker for this. We will also need a better GSM Shield for this.

Sending an SMS

In this section, we will learn how we can send an SMS using our GSM Shield and Arduino. To send an SMS, we will use AT Commands once more. It is almost similar to the method used when calling with the GSM Shield.

Since we know how we can configure the GSM Shield and the Arduino, we will skip this part and go straight to the coding.

We need to include the `SoftwareSerial` library as we did before.

This time we will first set our GSM to be ready to send a text message. We can do this by printing the following line on the `GSM.println()` function:

```
GSMSerial.println("AT+CMGF=1");
```

Here, the AT+CMGF=1 command will set the GSM Shield to text mode. It is something similar to the Boolean operation – 1 can be replaced with 0 if we want to disable the text mode. It is a good practice to wait few moments after sending a command to the GSM Shield. We will wait 1 second, so we need to write `delay(1000);` after the `GSMSerial.println();` command.

Now we will set the phone number to which we want to send the SMS by the following command:

```
GSMSerial.println("AT+CMGS="+#############"\r");
```

Here, ############# is the phone number. We will again wait for 1 second by declaring delay(1000) after the previous command. We need to send a text to the number we used. We can write the text by writing the following line where **"Hello Arduino!!"** is the text we want to send to the phone number:

```
GSMSerial.println("Hello Arduino!!");
```

We will again wait 1 second by calling the dealy() function .

Finally, we need to send a signal to the GSM Shield that our text message ends, and we are confirming the text to be sent. To do this we need to press CTRL+Zon the keyboard, but we will use the ASCII value of the CTRL+Z and send it to the GSM Shield. The ASCII value of *CTRL + Zis 26*, so we will write `GSMSerial.println((char)26);`

The full version of the code for sending a text to a number is as follows:

```
#include <SoftwareSerial.h>
SoftwareSerial GSMSerial(2, 3);
void setup() {
  Serial.begin(9600);
  Serial.println("Warming Up the GSM Shield; Look at the Shield's LED");
  Serial.println("..........");
  Serial.println("...............");
  Serial.println(".....................");
  Serial.println("..........................");
  GSMSerial.begin(9600);
  delay(1000);
  GSMSerial.println("AT+CMGF=1");      //Sets the GSM Shield to Text Mode
  delay(1000);   // Wait 1 second
  GSMSerial.println("AT+CMGS="+#############"\r");// Replace
############# with mobile number
  delay(1000);
  GSMSerial.println("Hello Arduino!!");// The SMS text you want to send
  delay(100);
  GSMSerial.println((char)26);// ASCII code of CTRL+Z
```

```
    delay(1000);
    Serial.println("Sucessfully sent your text!"); // Printing a success
message on the Serial Monitor.
    }

void loop() {


}
```

Now we will run the code and see if we receive a text:

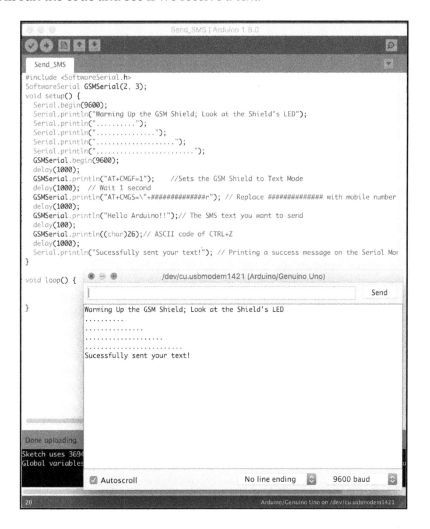

The output says the text we wanted to send was sent. Let's check if we really got it:

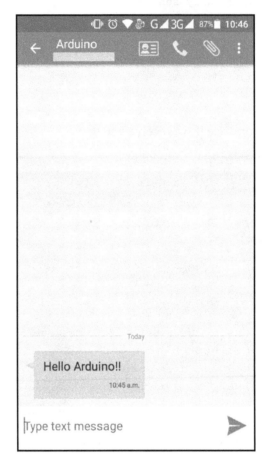

Yes! I got an SMS from the SIM I used on the GSM Shield with the text I wanted to send!

Receiving an SMS

In this section, we will learn how we can receive an SMS using our GSM Shield and Arduino. We will display the SMS on the Serial Monitor.

To receive an SMS and display it on the Serial Monitor, we need to use the SoftwareSerial library. Receiving an SMS is simpler than sending an SMS. We just need to make the GSM Shield understand that the Shield is working and ready to receive a text.

To make the GSM Shield ready for receiving a text message, the command we should use is the following:

GSMSerial.println("AT+CNMI=2,2,0,0,0");

We can assign the received SMS to a string variable and print it on the Serial Monitor.

The full source code for receiving text messages is as follows:

```
#include <SoftwareSerial.h>
SoftwareSerial GSMSerial(2, 3);
void setup() {
  String text;
  Serial.begin(9600);
  Serial.println("Warming Up the GSM Shield; Look at the Shield's LED");
  Serial.println(".........");
  Serial.println("..............");
  Serial.println("...................");
  Serial.println(".........................");
  GSMSerial.begin(9600);
  text = GSMSerial.println("AT+CNMI=2,2,0,0,0");
  delay(1000);
  Serial.println("Received a text message.");
  Serial.println("The Message is: ");
  Serial.println(text);
}

void loop() {

}
```

Now run the code, and send a text to the number of the SIM used on the GSM Shield.

I have sent an SMS to the SIM used on the GSM Shield. My text was **Hello my Arduino!**

Yes! We received the text we sent!

Summary

In this chapter, we have learned a lot of things. We learned the characteristics of OOPs and we learned how to configure a GSM Shield with the Arduino board. This chapter is one of the most important chapters if you want to improve your use of the microcontroller and OOPs concepts. I do not recommend that you skip this chapter. If you feel this chapter is hard, try to study and do the exercises in a silent environment and do the electrical parts with caution. You might get a number of errors. Don't feel disappointed; just move to `Chapter 10`, *Few Error Handlings*. I hope this chapter won't be that hard for you. You will find a number of solutions to the problems you might find while working with the GSM Shield and Arduino. In the next chapter, we will learn two interesting thing-pointers and structure of C programming.

7

Using Pointers and Structure

In this chapter, we will learn about pointers and structure of C programming using Arduino. We had a brief introduction to the pointer in the preceding chapter, while learning about the characteristics of object-oriented programming. This chapter will be a detailed discussion of pointers, reference points, and a new thing: structure. We will also discuss pointer types, pointers and arrays, how can we use pointers, use of structure, and so on. So, let's start our journey.

Pointers

Well, from the preceding chapter, you might remember the definition of pointers. Let's recap so that we can look at a better definition and learn about the usages of pointers.

You already know that a variable holds data. Say, an integer holds an integer number, a string holds a collection of characters, or a float holds a floating-point number. Each of the data types holds different types of data. Pointers are kind of similar to the variables, but they hold the memory location. Let's make it clear.

The variables hold information. The information is saved somewhere in our computer or Arduino. The information can be anywhere in our computer or Arduino. By declaring a pointer, we can find exactly where the variable is saved.

To make our definition shorter, we can say a pointer is just a variable, as in `int`, `char`, `float`, `double`, and so on.

Say, a box is like a variable. In a box, we can put things. So, a box can have some space. In programming, we may call it memory. Every variable has a memory size of 8, 16, or 32 bits. Let's define an integer, `myVar` as follows:

```
int myVar;
```

Now, the system assigned 16/32-bit memory for the variable. We can assign `myVar` with any value within the limits (How long number an integer can store).

We will assign `12` to `myVar` as follows:

```
int myVar = 12;
```

For now, let's compare the memory of the Arduino with a lot of boxes. Say each box has a number. Since all the boxes are kept in a location, when necessary, we need to find out where they are. So, if we give a number to each of the boxes, we can find the box in no time. If we find our desired box, then finding the objects inside the box is much easier.

That is the main gist of a pointer. Let's find out a little bit more.

Declaring a pointer

When declaring a pointer, you must initialize with some valid value. Otherwise, we will get a null pointer error. We will discuss null pointers in more detail later.

To declare a pointer, we need to use an asterisk (`*`) in between the type of the pointer and the name of the pointer. Say our pointer name is `myPointer` and the type is integer; we can declare our pointer as follows:

```
int *myPointer;
```

or,

```
int* myPointer;
```

or,

```
int * myPointer;
```

Remember, `myPointer` is not an address; it is just a variable to store an address.

As previously mentioned, our `myVar` is an integer and its value is `12`. If we want to get `myVar`'s address, all we need to do is put an ampersand (`&`) symbol before it. So, the address of `myVar` is `&myVar`. We can now store `myVar`'s address to a pointer, as follows:

```
myPointer = &myVar;
```

If we print the value of `myPointer` now, we will get the address where the integer is saved.

Let's test the thing by writing the following code inside our `setup()` function:

```
int myVar = 12; // Our integer
int *myPointer; // Our Pointer
myPointer = &myVar; // Assigned address to the pointer
```

Now we will print the value of `myPointer` in hexadecimal format. Since we do not know the numerical length of the address of `myVar`, we will cast our pointer to `long`. So, let's print the address as follows:

```
Serial.println((long)myPointer, HEX);
```

After compiling and uploading the code to our Arduino, we will get a result similar to the following (your output might depend on the microcontroller of the Arduino board):

In my case, the output is **21F9**. This is a hexadecimal number. This is the location where the `myVar` is saved. Let's retrieve what is at the address **21F9**. To find out what is at the address, we will print it by adding an asterisk (*) before the `myPointer`; this time, this is not a hexadecimal number, it is a decimal number. Using the asterisk to retrieve the value contained in the pointed address is called **dereferencing**. Let's look at the full source code and the output:

```
void setup() {
  int myVar = 12;
  int *myPointer;
  myPointer = &myVar;
  Serial.begin(9600);
  Serial.print("Address : ");
  Serial.println((long)myPointer, HEX); // To find the address
  Serial.print("Value: ");
  Serial.print((long)*myPointer); // To see what is on the address
}

void loop() {

}
```

Yes, the address is 21F9, and on the address, we found an integer, 12.

Reference point

We have already used an ampersand (&) to find the address of a variable. This ampersand is called a reference operator. To get the address of a variable, we will use this reference operator. We assigned the value of &myVar to myPointer just a moment ago, writing myPointer = &myVar; well, this means we stored the value of the address of myVar to our pointer, myPointer.

Types of pointers

Interestingly people say there is only one type of pointer, a memory address. But pointers can point to any type, so we can say, there is an infinite number of different types of pointers. In C programming, we use a number of pointers. A few of them are as follows:

- Integer pointers
- Character pointers
- Double pointers
- Long pointers
- Void pointers

If we distinguish pointers by their nature, we can classify them as follows:

- **Null pointers**: Null pointers point to the address zero, which does not point to a function or an object. NULL is a macro constant that can be defined as how we include a library:

```
#define NULL 0
```

We can declare a null pointer as follow:

```
int *myPointerInt = (int *)0;
int *myPointerInteger = NULL;
double *myPointerDouble = (double *)0;
char *myPointerChar = '';
char *myPointerCharacter = (char *)0;
float *myPointerFloat = (float *)0;
```

Your simple task is to print all the values of the pointers (null pointer) and understand the output.

- **Wild pointer**: Pointers that are not initialized in our program are known as wild pointers.

- **Complex pointers**: Complex pointers are different types of pointers, as follows:
  - Pointer to an array
  - Pointer to a function
  - Pointer to a structure
  - Pointer to a union
  - Multilevel pointer
  - We will skip this type of pointer for now. We will look at some examples when we learn about structure.
- **Dangling pointers**: Dangling pointers are similar to wild pointers. Even if, at some stage, they pointed to something, that something went out of scope and now they do not point to any function or object. Look at the following code:

```
void setup() {
  char *myPointer = NULL;
  {
    char myVar;
    myPointer = &myVar;
  }
  //myPointer is now a Dangling pointer
}
```

- **Generic pointers**: When a variable is declared as a pointer that is a void type, we can call the variable or pointer a generic pointer. Simply put, a void-type pointer is a generic pointer. A generic pointer cannot be dereferenced. Look at the following code:

```
void setup() {
..int myVar;
..void *myPointer; // A Generic Pointer.
..myPointer = &myVar;
}
```

Now that we know about pointers, let's find out where we can use them.

Pointers and arrays

Pointers not only store the addresses of the variables; they also hold the address of a cell of an array. Look at the following code:

```
void setup() {
  int myVar[5] = {1, 3, 5, 6, 8};
  int *myPointer;
```

```
  myPointer = &myVar[0];
// &myVar[0] is the address of the 1st element of myVar[5]
}
```

Say we need to print the third element of our array. In the preceding code, `myPointer` holds the value of the first element of our array. So, to access the third element, we need to increment our pointer by 2, as follows:

```
myPointer = myPointer+2;
```

Now, if we print `myPointer` value, we will get the third element of our array. Let's look at what our program and output will be for that case:

```
void setup() {
  int *myPointer;
  int myVar[5] = {1, 3, 5, 6, 8};
  myPointer = &myVar[0]; // Holds the address of the 1st element.
  myPointer = myPointer + 2;
// Incremented by 2 to get 3rd value of our array.
  Serial.begin(9600);
  Serial.print(*myPointer);
}
```

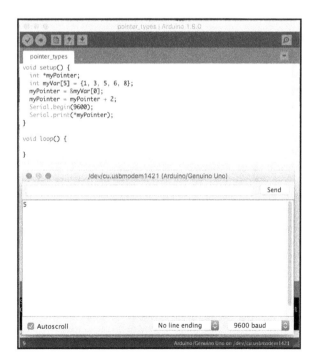

We can access any element by using pointers. Let's print all the elements of the array by using pointers:

```
void setup() {
  int *myPointer;
  int myVar[5] = {1, 3, 5, 6, 8};
  Serial.begin(9600);
  myPointer = &myVar[0];
  myPointer = myPointer + 0;
  Serial.println(*myPointer);
  myPointer = &myVar[0]; //Reset the address
  myPointer = myPointer + 1;
  Serial.println(*myPointer);
  myPointer = &myVar[0];
  myPointer = myPointer + 2;
  Serial.println(*myPointer);
  myPointer = &myVar[0];
  myPointer = myPointer + 3;
  Serial.println(*myPointer);
  myPointer = &myVar[0];
  myPointer = myPointer + 4;
  Serial.println(*myPointer);

}

void loop() {

}
```

The output of the code will be as follows:

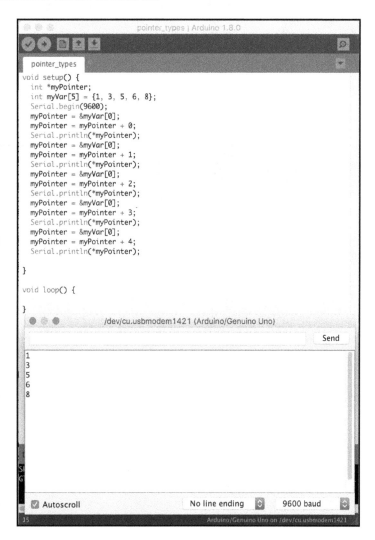

We can also print the array using a loop, as follows:

```
void setup() {
  int *myPointer;
  int myVar[5] = {1, 3, 5, 6, 8};
  Serial.begin(9600);
  myPointer = &myVar[0];
  for (int i = 0; i < 5; i++) {
    myPointer = myPointer + i; //incremented as the value of i
```

```
        Serial.println(*myPointer);
        myPointer = &myVar[0]; //Reset the pointer
    }
}

void loop() {

}
```

The output will be also the same:

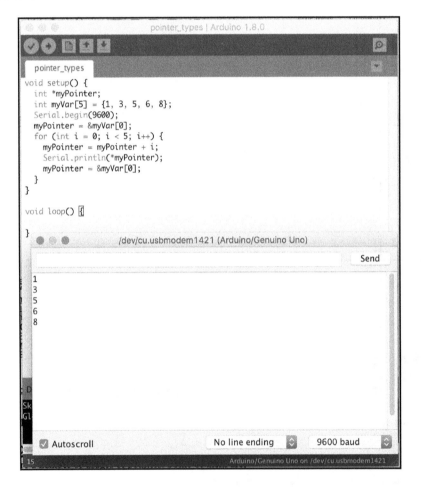

Let's print both the addresses of all the elements and their values. Look at the following code:

```
void setup() {
  int *myPointer;
  int myVar[5] = {1, 3, 5, 6, 8};
  Serial.begin(9600);
  myPointer = &myVar[0];
  Serial.println("Values of the elements: ");
  for (int i = 0; i < 5; i++) {
    myPointer = myPointer + i;
    Serial.print("myVar[");
    Serial.print(i);
    Serial.print("] = ");
    Serial.println(*myPointer);
    myPointer = &myVar[0];
  }
  Serial.println("Addresses of the elements: ");
  for (int i = 0; i < 5; i++) {
    myPointer = myPointer + i; // Incremented the pointer
    Serial.print("myPointer + ");
    Serial.print(i);
    Serial.print(" = ");
    Serial.println((long)myPointer, HEX); // Prints the address
    myPointer = &myVar[0];
  }
}

void loop() {

}
```

The output of the preceding code will be as follows:

From the output, we can see that the address of the pointers incremented by 0, 1, 2, and 4:

myPointer + 0 = 8F2

myPointer + 1 = 8F4

myPointer + 2 = 8F8

myPointer + 3 = 8FE

myPointer + 4 = 906

Can you say why? Yes, it is because each integer occupies two bytes of memory.

In a nutshell:

- `&myVar[0]` is equal to `myPointer` and `*myPointer` is equal to `myVar[0]`
- `&myVar[1]` is equal to `myPointer+1` and `*(myPointer+1)` is equal to `myVar[1]`
- `&myVar[3]` is equal to `myPointer+3` and `*(myPointer+3)` is equal to `myVar[3]`
- `&myVar[i]` is equal to `myPointer+i` and `*(myPointer+i)` is equal to `myVar[i]`

Usages of pointers

There are a number of usages for pointers. Some of them are as follows:

- We can access the Arduino memory directly by using pointers
- Pointer reduce memory wastage
- Pointers reduce the complexity of a program
- Pointers return more than one value to a function
- Pointers create an alternative way to access the array elements
- By using pointers, we can extract the address of objects
- Pointers help to build a complex data structure
- Pointers allow us to perform dynamic memory allocation
- Pointers allow us to resize the dynamic memory allocation

- Pointers reduce the execution time of a program
- Array handling is much easier when we work with pointers
- Since the pointers return a number, if our program deals with strings and characters, it becomes easy for us to manipulate the program

We will now discuss another interesting thing, called structure.

Learning about structure

We learned about arrays previously. An array holds elements of the same type of data. Say, an integer type of array holds only integers, or a character type of array holds only characters. But a structure is something that can hold different types of data together. To define a structure in C, we can say that a structure is a collection of variables of different data types.

Let's say we want to store information about a person, such as their name, PhoneNum, sex, and salary. All this information is not of the same type. name is a string, PhoneNum is an integer, sex can be defined by a character, and salary is a double number. So, defining one array to store them is not possible. We need to know something else that can hold multiple types of variables. To make the problem even complex, say we want to store information about multiple people.

Can you visualize how messy and long the code we will have to write will be if we want to work with an ordinary array? Well, we will use a structure to avoid the messiness. The basic syntax of a structure in C is as follows:

```
struct structName {
    //information
    //variables
};
```

Here, struct is the keyword by which we will start writing our structure. Then we will need to declare the name of the structure. Inside the parentheses, we will declare our different types of variables. For the preceding scenario about storing information about a person, we can write our structure as follows:

```
struct personInfo {
    String name;
    int PhoneNum;
    char sex;
    double salary;
};
```

We can declare a structure before our `setup()` function, or inside the `setup()` or `loop()` function, depending on what we want to do. It is a good practice to declare a structure outside the `setup()` or `loop()` function.

 Do not forget to use the semicolon (;) after declaring a structure.

To store information to the variables we declared inside the parentheses (`name`, `phoneNum`, `sex`, and `salary`), we use the dot "." operator. We can either take input from the Serial Monitor, or write it as follows.

First, we need to define a structure for a person. Say it is `person1`:

```
personInfo person1; //Declared person1
person1.name = "John"; //A string variable
person1.PhoneNum = 12345; //An integer
person1.sex = 'M'; //A character
person1.salary = 120590.30;//a double
```

For `person2`, we can store information as follows:

```
personInfo person2; //Declared person2
person2.name = "Jen";
person2.PhoneNum = 8765;
person2.sex = 'F';
person2.salary = 21000.50;
```

To print any of the information, all you have to do is print the variable as follows (for `person1`):

```
Serial.println(person1.name);
Serial.println(person1.PhoneNum);
Serial.println(person1.sex);
Serial.println(person1.salary);
```

Let's look at the output for a clearer idea of printing the information of a structure:

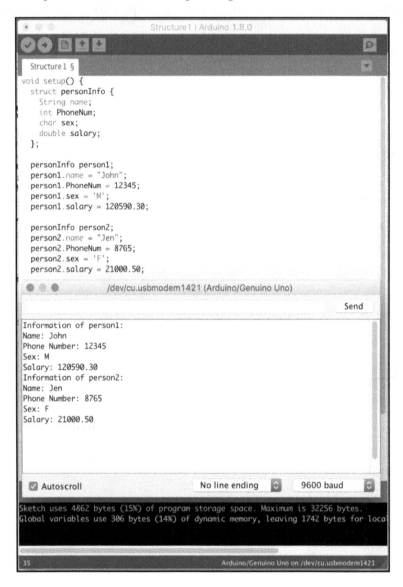

If you look at the full source code of the program executed in the preceding screenshot, you can clearly understand what happened in the code. So, here is the code:

```
void setup() {
  struct personInfo {//This is our structure
    String name;
    int PhoneNum;
    char sex;
    double salary;
  };

  personInfo person1; //Declared values of the variables for  person1
  person1.name = "John";
  person1.PhoneNum = 12345;
  person1.sex = 'M';
  person1.salary = 120590.30;

  personInfo person2; //Declared values of the variables for  person2
  person2.name = "Jen";
  person2.PhoneNum = 8765;
  person2.sex = 'F';
  person2.salary = 21000.50;

  Serial.begin(9600);
  Serial.println("Information of person1: ");//Printed person1  info
  Serial.print("Name: ");
  Serial.println(person1.name);
  Serial.print("Phone Number: ");
  Serial.println(person1.PhoneNum);
  Serial.print("Sex: ");
  Serial.println(person1.sex);
  Serial.print("Salary: ");
  Serial.println(person1.salary);

  Serial.println("Information of person2: ");//Printed person1   info
  Serial.print("Name: ");
  Serial.println(person2.name);
  Serial.print("Phone Number: ");
  Serial.println(person2.PhoneNum);
  Serial.print("Sex: ");
  Serial.println(person2.sex);
  Serial.print("Salary: ");
  Serial.println(person2.salary);
}

void loop() {

}
```

Structure and function

Structure and function are two different things in C programming. We can pass the values of a structure to a function to make our program shorter and more efficient. There are two ways to pass a structure to a function: pass by value and pass by reference. First we will look at pass by value.

Pass by value

To pass a structure to a function, first we need to define a structure. Say we will define a structure Box, where we will have three double variables: length, height, and width:

```
struct Box { //declared Box structure
   float height; //height of the box
   float width; //width of the box
   float length; //length of the box
};
```

Now, we will build a function that calculates the volume of a box and prints it on the Serial Monitor:

```
void volume(struct Box box) { //Passed Structure
   double volume = box.height * box.width * box.length;  //calculation
   Serial.print("The volume of the box is ");
   Serial.println(volume); //Printed volume
}
```

In the preceding function, we have passed our structure (struct Box). We passed it with a variable name (box), which is a temporary variable for the function. Inside the function, we have used this variable to call the members of the structure with a period (.), as we did before.

`box.height` will fetch the value of the height from the structure, which will be initialized in the `setup()` function as follows:

```
Box box1; //Declared a temporary object for box1
box1.height = 5.5; //Height of box1
box1.width = 3.5; //width of box1
box1.length = 2.2; //length of box1
```

Finally, we need to call our `volume();` function with the temporary object we just created, as follows:

```
volume(box1);
```

The full code of the program and output are as follows:

```
struct Box { //Our structure
   float height;
   float width;
   float length;
};
void volume(struct Box box) { //our function
   double volume = box.height * box.width * box.length;
   Serial.print("The volume of the box is ");
   Serial.println(volume);
}
void setup() {

   Serial.begin(9600);
   Box box1;
   box1.height = 5.5;
   box1.width = 3.5;
   box1.length = 2.2;
   volume(box1); //Called the function
}

void loop() {


}
```

Pass by reference

Since we have learned about pointers, we can pass our structure to a function by using the memory address. This method of passing a structure by the memory address is known as a pass by reference. Let's define a structure first:

```
struct student { // defined a structure with three variables
    String name;
    int age;
    int roll;
};
```

Now we will write our function to print the personal information of a student. This time, we will pass a pointer to the function, and the information will not be copied in a temporary variable, but the function will access the information of a previously created variable with the pointer. This time we will not use the dot . operator but the arrow -> operator:

```
void showInfo(struct student *std) { //passed pointer
    Serial.print("Name: ");
    Serial.println(std->name); //printed the value of the address
    Serial.print("Age: ");
    Serial.println(std->age);
    Serial.print("Roll: ");
    Serial.println(std->roll);

}
```

 Note that "std->age" is the same as (*std) age, the arrow operator is a shortcut.

When we call the showInfo() function, we need to pass our structure as a pointer. We first need to declare the variables for a student. For student1, we declare variables as follows:

```
student student1; //Created an object of the structure
student1.name = "John"; //declared name
student1.age = 16; //declared age
student1.roll = 5; //declared roll
```

To pass the values of `student1` to our function, we need to call the function as follows:

```
showInfo(&student1);
```

The full code of the pass by reference with output is given as follows:

```
struct student { //our structure
  String name;
  int age;
  int roll;
};

void showInfo(struct student *std) { //our function to pass pointer
  Serial.print("Name: ");
  Serial.println(std->name);
  Serial.print("Age: ");
  Serial.println(std->age);
  Serial.print("Roll: ");
  Serial.println(std->roll);

}

void setup() {
  Serial.begin(9600);
  student student1;
  student1.name = "John";
  student1.age = 16;
  student1.roll = 5;
  showInfo(&student1); //called the function.
}

void loop() {


}
```

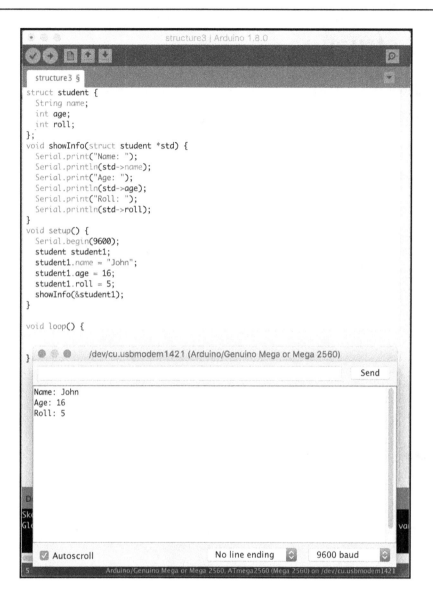

Nested structure

We can declare a nested structure as the nested loop. This means we can define a structure inside another structure. The basic syntax of a nested structure is as follows:

```
struct firstStructure { // our first structure
  //variables
};
struct secondStructure { // Our second structure
  struct firstStruct objName; //Created object of fist  structure(Nesting)
  //More variables
};
```

Let's look at an example. Let's say we need two types of information about a student, basic information and personal information. The basic information includes the name and roll number. The personal information includes age, phoneNum and sex. The structures of the two types of information will be as follows:

```
struct basicInfo { // our first structure
  String name;
  int roll;
};
struct personalInfo { //our second structure.
  int age;
  int phoneNum;
  char sex;
};
```

We will nest the first structure to the second structure by creating an object of the first structure inside the second structure, as follows:

```
struct basicInfo baseInfo;
```

So, the personalInfo structure will look like as follows:

```
struct personalInfo {
  struct basicInfo baseInfo;
  int age;
  int phoneNum;
  char sex;
};
```

Declaring variables one by one is too time consuming, so this time, we will declare all the variables in a single line. Follow the code given here:

```
struct personalInfo information = {"John", 5, 16, 1234, 'M'};
```

Look carefully; we have created an object of the second structure (`information`) and created an array-like thing where we added values to the variables we declared inside both our structures. Please note that the order of writing the array-like thing must be the same as the structures variables sequential order. Since we have created an object inside the `personalInfo` structure (`baseInfo`), we need to assign values to the `basicInfo` structures variables first, inside the array-like thing. If we want to access any variable from the first structure, we need to write the following:

```
secondStructureObject.firstStructureObject.VariableName;
```

In our case, if we want to print the name of the `student`, we need to access it by writing `information.baseInfo.name;`

Let's print the values of the variables on the Serial Monitor, as follows:

```
struct basicInfo {
  String name;
  int roll;
};
struct personalInfo {
  struct basicInfo baseInfo;
  int age;
  int phoneNum;
  char sex;
};

void setup() {
  Serial.begin(9600);
  struct personalInfo information = {"John", 5, 16, 1234, 'M'};
  Serial.print("Name: ");
  Serial.println(information.baseInfo.name);
  Serial.print("Roll: ");
  Serial.println(information.baseInfo.roll);
  Serial.print("Age: ");
  Serial.println(information.age);
  Serial.print("Phone Number: ");
  Serial.println(information.phoneNum);
  Serial.print("Sex: ");
  Serial.println(information.sex);

}
```

```
void loop() {

}
```

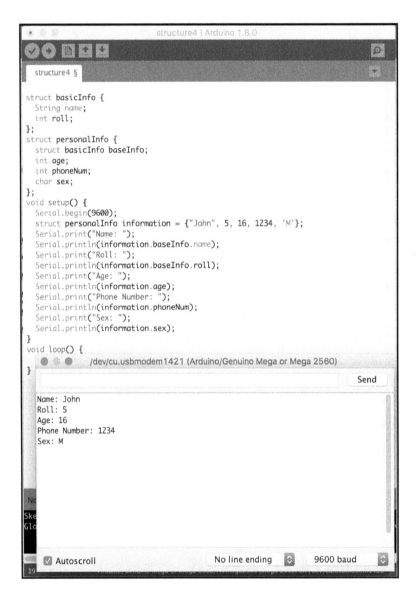

Exercise

- Take an input from the Serial Monitor, and display the value on the Serial Monitor using a pointer.
- Using structure, write a program to print all the values of the structure by using a pointer and array.
- Write a program with three structures (basicInfo, personalInfo and extendedInfo), with a number of variables. Print them from the setup() class as shown on the nested structure, but this time, use a pointer.
- Store five values to an array by using a pointer and print them using a loop.

Summary

We have learned two confusing and great aspects of C programming in this chapter. The pointer is very useful for memory saving, since we are working with a small-memory device. A structure helps to organize and shorten our code. If we want to learn coding efficiently, we must not skip this chapter, because this chapter will help us to prepare for Chapter 8, *Working with Arduino Libraries*.

8
Working with Arduino Libraries

In this chapter, we will learn about Arduino libraries. By the end of this chapter, you will know how to install Arduino libraries, manage libraries, and you'll also know a few famous features of Arduino libraries. In this chapter, we will also work with LCD boards and Servo. We already have a basic idea of what Arduino libraries are, but before going any further, we will learn more about them. We will also learn how we can make our own Arduino library.

Arduino library

We already know that a library is a collection of files. In programming, a library is a bunch of precompiled code that can be reused in many programs. In a library, there are things known as modules. Modules are stored in object format. The code of a library can be a function or a collection of functions, classes, variables, and so on. A library helps to interact with a particular task of an OS. In our case, an Arduino library does a particular job for the Arduino's microcontroller. The question is, why do we need libraries?

Well, if we didn't have libraries, remember what we had to include in our code for the SD file handling? Yes, we included `SD.h` library to our code. If you look inside the SD library, you will see a bunch of files similar to what is shown in the following screenshot (in a later section I will explain how you can go to the `library` folder of the Arduino IDE):

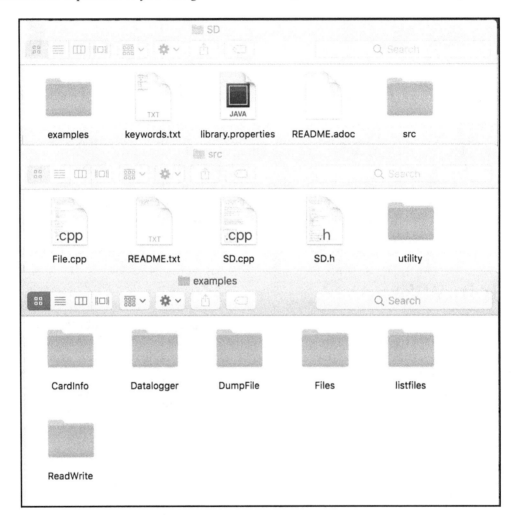

The basic structure of the files and folders of our SD library is as follows:

- SD Library:
- Examples (folder)
- CardInfo(folder):
- CardInfo.ino

- Datalogger(folder):
- Datalogger.ino
- DumpFile(folder):
- Dumpfile.ino
- Files(folder):
- Files.ino
- Listfiles(folder):
- Listfiles.ino
- ReadWrite(folder):
- ReadWrite.ino
- Keywords.txt
- Library.properties
- README.adoc
- src (folder):
- File.cpp
- README.txt
- SD.cpp
- SD.h
- Utility(folder):
- FatStructs.h
- Sd2Card.cpp
- Sd2Card.h
- Sd2PinMap.h
- SdFat.h
- SdFatmainpage.h
- SdFatUtil.h
- SdFile.cpp
- SdInfo.h
- SdVolume.cpp

Before going any further, let's find out the location of the pre-installed libraries of our Arduino IDE.

In Windows

To find the path of the library in Windows, follows these steps:

1. Firstly, you need to go to the root folder of your system (usually C drive).
2. Then go to `Program Files/Program Files (x86)/Arduino/libraries`.

See the following screenshot for a clear idea about the path of the library of Arduino IDE:

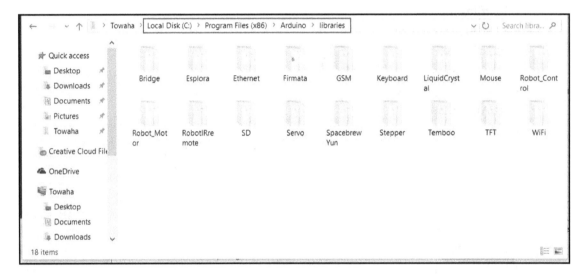

In OSX

After downloading the Arduino:

1. You may place it in the `Application` folder.
2. Go to the directory where you have the `Arduino.app` file.

3. Right-click on the app icon (two finger tap). You will see a list of options, as shown in the following screenshot:

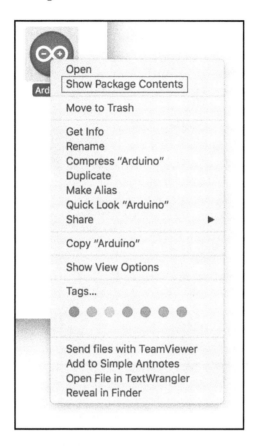

1. Click on the **Show Package Contents**.
2. Go to **Contents** | **Java** | **libraries**.

See the following screenshot with the entire `libraries` folder:

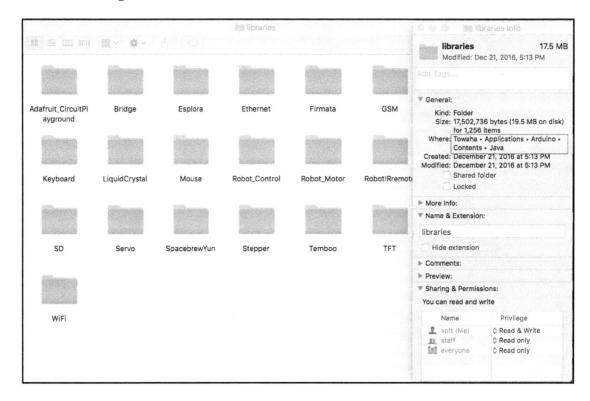

Linux OS

On Linux OS, the library folder's path can differ depending on the installation of the Arduino IDE. If you have installed it by downloading the arduino-VersionNunmer-`linux64.tar.xz` file and the command with `./install.sh` then the library folder is on the extracted folder. If you have installed Arduino IDE via the `apt-get install arduino` command, then the folder is on `/usr/share/arduino/libraries`.

See the following screenshot for a clear idea about the Arduino library path in Linux OS:

Now that we know the location of the `libraries` folder, we will learn what files are placed inside a library.

On Arduino IDE, we have the following libraries preinstalled:

- Adafruit_CircuitPlayground
- Bridge
- Esplora
- Ethernet
- Firmata
- GSM
- Keyboard
- LiquidCrystal
- Mouse
- Robot_Control
- Robot_Motor
- RobotIRremote
- SD
- Servo
- SpacebrewYun
- Stepper

- Temboo
- TFT
- WiFi

In this chapter, we will learn more details about `Servo`, `Firmata`, `SoftwareSerial`, `LiquidCrystal`, and `Stepper` libraries.

Types of libraries

Arduino IDE has two types of libraries:

- **Standard Libraries**: We already saw that a few libraries are preinstalled with the Arduino IDE. They come with the IDE and they support all the examples of the code given with the IDE. You may find the Arduino example code if you go to **File | Example**. See the following screenshot:

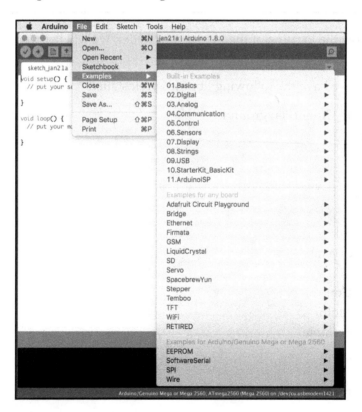

The standard libraries functions include the basic communication functions and they support some common hardware (for example, LED, Servo, GSM, SD card, Stepper motors, and so on).

- **User Installed Libraries**: In Arduino IDE, we can install our own libraries if needed. We can also make our own libraries and install them as needed. These libraries that do not come with the Arduino IDE are known as user installable libraries.

Some of the famous user installable libraries for the Arduino are as follows:

- DateTime
- Metro
- PString
- Tone
- FFT
- XBee
- SerialControl

We will learn how to install custom libraries on the Arduino IDE later.

Let's look at a few famous libraries that come with the Arduino IDE. We will discuss their functions and usages too.

The Servo library

You probably know what electric motors are. Electric motors transform electrical energy into mechanical energy. There are different types of electric motors on the market. They can be of different shapes, sizes, functions, efficiency, and purposes. The following image shows different types of motors with their names.

Servo is a special type of electric motor. We use Servo motors to specifically run a motor in certain directions and motions. We can control a Servo motor using Arduino Digital pin. By sending a signal to the Servo from the Arduino, we can control a Servo.

The following image shows a servo:

A Servo Motor

The Servo motor has the following three wires:

- Positive (Red Wire)
- Negative/Ground (Black/Brown Wire)
- Signal (Orange/Yellow/White Wire)

A Servo can be used by using the `servo` library. Let's run our Servo for the first time.

To run the Servo, we first need to connect it to the Arduino as follows:

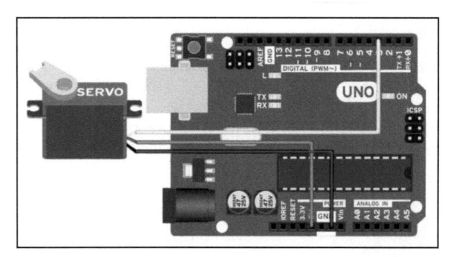

In our code, we will use pin 3 for sending signals to the Servo. You can use any digital pin of the Arduino board. So the Orange/Yellow (Signal) wire will be connected to the Arduino pin 3. The red wire (positive) will be connected to the 5v pin of the Arduino. And lastly, the Black wire (negative) will be connected to the GND pin of the Arduino. In a nutshell, the pin setup of the Servo and Arduino board is as follows:

Arduino Pin	Servo Wire
3	Signal Wire (Orange/Yellow)
5v	Positive Wire (Red)
GND	Negative Wire (Black)

Exploring Servo.h library

Now, let's fire up the Arduino and then open the Arduino IDE. Since we are working with the servo library, firstly, we need to include our servo library to the code:

```
#include <Servo.h>
```

Then we will define our Servo on our code as follows:

```
Servo myServo; // Here you can use any name
```

Inside the setup() function we will write our code to move our Servo 90 degrees anticlockwise. Before that, we need to declare our pin on which we have connected the Servo signal pin:

```
void setup()
{
  myServo.attach(3);
  myServo.write(90);  //This will move the Servo 90 degree anticlockwise
}
```

If we want to move our Servo clockwise, all we need to do is place a negative sign(-) before 90:

```
myServo.write(-90);  //This will move the Servo 90 degree clockwise
```

Our Servo can move 180 degrees in total. There are also some Servo motors that can move 360 degrees in total.

Let's say we want our Servo to move clockwise 90 degrees first and then 90 degrees clockwise. Our full code will be as follows:

```
#include <Servo.h>

Servo myServo;

void setup()
{
  myServo.attach(3);
  myServo.write(90);
  delay(1000); // This will give 1 second rest to the servo.
  myServo.write(-90);

}

void loop() {
}
```

Knob the Servo

You may have seen some radio buttons that allow you to turn on some device. The following figure shows a knob in case you do not know. It can be turned both clockwise and anticlockwise. Now we will code for our Servo to use it with a knob, so that when we will turn the knob (to whatever direction), the Servo will turn in the same direction:

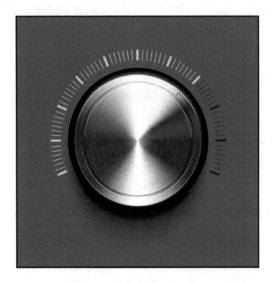

To use our Servo with a knob we will need a potentiometer. The following image shows different kinds of potentiometers:

We will use the potentiometer as our knob. Let's connect the potentiometer and the Servo with the Arduino, as shown in the following figure:

In short, the pin mappings are:

- Servo Signal (Orange/Yellow wire) -Arduino Pin 3
- Servo Ground (Black/Brown Wire) -Arduino Pin GND
- Servo Positive (Red wire) -Arduino Pin 5V
- Potentiometer middle pin-Arduino Pin A0
- Potentiometer left pin -Arduino Pin Common with Servo Ground
- Potentiometer right pin- Arduino Pin Common with Servo Positive

Now that we have connected our Servo and Potentiometer to the Arduino, let's write code now.

We do not need to write the code for now, because we already have the code in the example code section of our Arduino IDE.

Let's import the code from the example menu of the Arduino IDE. To do this, we need to go to **File** | **Examples** | **Servo** | **Knob**. See the following screenshot for a better understanding:

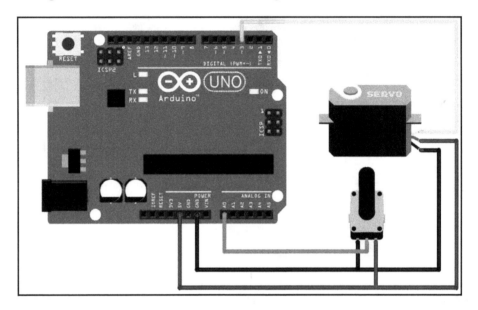

Our Knob code will look as follows:

```
#include <Servo.h>

Servo myservo;  // create servo object to control a servo

int potpin = 0;  // analog pin used to connect the potentiometer
int val;     // variable to read the value from the analog pin

void setup() {
  myservo.attach(9);  // attaches the servo on pin 9 to the servo object
}

void loop() {
  val = analogRead(potpin);            // reads the value of the
potentiometer (value between 0 and 1023)
  val = map(val, 0, 1023, 0, 180);     // scale it to use it with the servo
(value between 0 and 180)
  myservo.write(val);                  // sets the servo position according
to the scaled value
  delay(15);                           // waits for the servo to get there
}
```

The code is simple. We imported the `servo` library, declared our Servo, and then we initialized two integers. I will discuss them in a moment. Inside the `setup()` function we declared the pin on which we have connected the signal pin of our Servo. In the code from the example, you may see the line with a `myservo.attach(9);` parameter. Change it to `myservo.attach(3);` as we have connected the signal pin to pin 3.

Inside the `loop()`, there are a few lines. The first line is for setting the value that comes from the potentiometer. The potentiometer's range is 0 to 1023. It means the potentiometer will convert the 180 degrees movement of the Servo into 1024 pieces. So, per signal from the potentiometer, the Servo will rotate roughly 0.176 degrees.

We have declared two integers (potpin and val). We have initialized the value of potpin to 0 because our potentiometer's middle pin is connected to A0.

Then we assigned the val to the value that comes from the pin **A0** as follows:

```
val = analogRead(potpin);
```

There is a `map()` function in the Arduino code that allows us to convert a number from one range to another and returns an integer value. We assigned the integer value to our val variable:

```
val = map(val, 0, 1023, 0, 180);
```

We compared our full rotation of the potentiometer with the Servo's full rotation. So we passed the initial and final values of the rotations of both Servo and potentiometer to the `map()` function.

Remember, we need to follow the preceding code because the `map()` function was written on its library as this.

And lastly we passed the value of val to the `myservo.write()` function. We kept a delay of 15 milliseconds for giving the Servo a little rest.

Please note that we have placed the code inside the `loop()` function, so this will run all the time after uploading it to the Arduino.

If we upload the code to the Arduino after connecting the Servo and the potentiometer we will be able to control the Servo from the potentiometer. If we rotate the potentiometer clockwise, our Servo will rotate clockwise and vice versa.

Sweep with Servo

Sweeping with Servo is much easier. We can also find the code in the example section of the Arduino IDE. The connection of the Servo and Arduino is as follows:

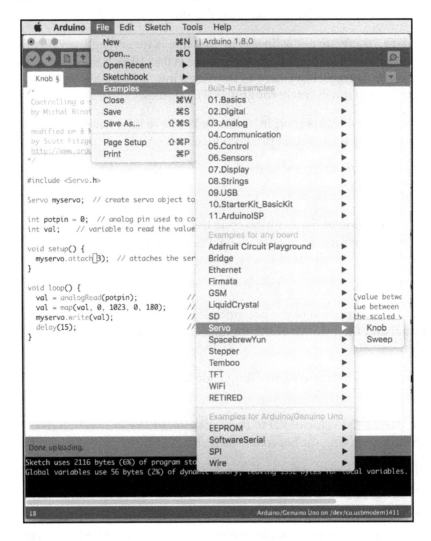

The Sweep code from the example is as follows:

```
#include <Servo.h>
Servo myservo;
int pos = 0;
void setup() {
```

```
myservo.attach(3);
}
void loop() {
for (pos = 0; pos <= 180; pos += 1) {
myservo.write(pos);
delay(15);
}
for (pos = 180; pos >= 0; pos -= 1) {
myservo.write(pos);
delay(15);
}
}
```

The first portion of the code is similar to the Knob code. All we changed is the pin number. From myservo.attach(9); to myservo.attach(3);. Inside the loop() function we have two for loops.

The first for loop will turn our Servo from 0 degrees to 180 degrees. The second for loop will turn the Servo from 180 degrees to 0 degrees. And this will occur for infinite time as they both are in the loop() function.

We have a pos integer declared on the top of the setup() function.

This variable will control the for loops. We passed the value of pos to myservo.write(pos); to both the loops. Then we delayed 15 milliseconds after each for loop to give the Servo a rest.

We initialized pos with 0, set a condition (greater than 180 or less than 180), and incremented by 1 every time on both the loops. We can rewrite the loop() function as follows, as we have learned about better incrementing:

```
void loop() {
for (pos = 0; pos <= 180; pos++) {
myservo.write(pos);
delay(15);
}
for (pos = 180; pos >= 0; pos--) {
myservo.write(pos);
delay(15);
}
}
```

The Firmata library

The Firmata library is an advanced level library to communicate with the Arduino microcontroller from the Arduino IDE on a computer. Simply, Firmata is a genetic protocol that enables any computer to take full control over a microcontroller (for example, Arduino). By using this library, we can decide what pins will be inputs and what pins will be the outputs. Basically we can control the Arduino pins to read the pins or set the pins to read any sensor such as buttons, potentiometers, light sensors, or PIR (Passive Infrared Sensor) sensors and we can control parts such as LEDs, relays, speakers, or Servo motors. In Firmata we do not need to write any code. We will see how we can import a simple Firmata code and run it to take control of the pins and onboard LEDs of the Arduino.

After opening the Arduino IDE, you need to go to **File** | **Examples** | **Firmata**. From there we can use the example code to take control over the Arduino and the sensors:

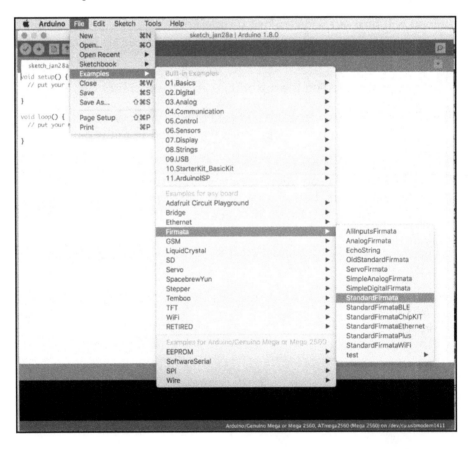

The SoftwareSerial library

There is a thing inside the microcontroller called **UART** (**Universal Asynchronous Receiver Transmitter**). It takes a byte and splits it into bits. Then it sends (one bit at a time) it over a communication channel. Before serial communication, we used to use parallel communication by which we could send a number of bits for a character at once at the same time. You might have seen the parallel communication wire or port. A parallel communication wire looks as follows:

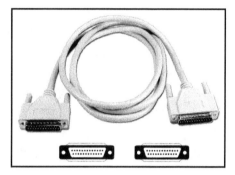

This is a pretty large port and it takes a large space on our computer, we Serial Communication was invented:

The serial communication can be done with any pin of the Arduino by using the `SoftwareSerial` library, or on pins 0 and 1 with the Serial class. We already used serial communication whenever we used the serial monitor, and also in the previous chapter while we worked with the GSM module. On our Arduino, the 0(Rx) and 1(Tx) pins are usually used for Serial Communication.

The LiquidCrystal library

Before going any further about the uses of `LiquidCrystal` library, we will first learn about displays that we can connect to our Arduino. We can connect a number of types of displays to an Arduino board. A few of them are shown in the following image:

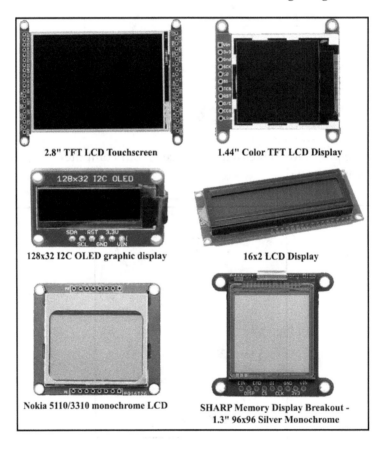

2.8" TFT LCD Touchscreen   1.44" Color TFT LCD Display

128x32 I2C OLED graphic display   16x2 LCD Display

Nokia 5110/3310 monochrome LCD   SHARP Memory Display Breakout -
1.3" 96x96 Silver Monochrome

We can use the touch screen displays or LCD displays. For avoiding complexities we will learn how we can use the LCD displays with the Arduino using the `LiquidCrystal` library.

The common LCD display board is 16×2 LCD display. The 16×2 LCD display looks as follows:

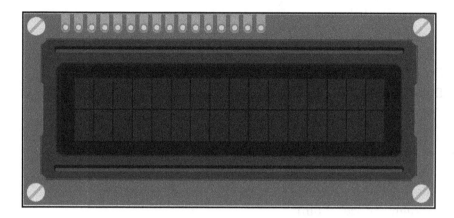

It has 16 pins. Each pin does a different task. The pin out of the display is as follows:

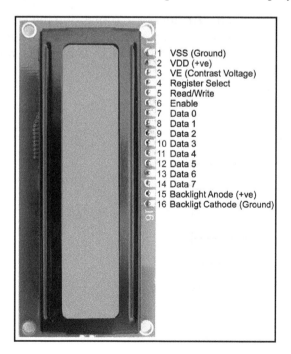

There are 16 pins of the LCD display, the pins are as follows:

- VSS (Ground Pin)
- VDD (3V/5V positive pin)
- VE (Display Contrast Pin) also known as the VO pin
- RS (Register Select Pin)
- Read/Write (RW pin)
- Enable Pin
- Data 0 pin
- Data 1 pin
- Data 2 pin
- Data 3 pin
- Data 4 pin
- Data 5 pin
- Data 6 pin
- Data 7 pin
- Backlight Anode (A pin)
- Backlight cathode (K pin)

Let's connect the LCD display to the Arduino. For connecting the LCD board to the Arduino we might need a potentiometer to adjust the brightness of the LCD. In the pinout of the display we have seen that there are 16 pins of the LCD display. The following table shows how we will connect them:

LCD Display Pin	Arduino Board Pin
RS	Pin 12
Enable	Pin 11
D4	Pin 5
D5	Pin 4
D6	Pin 3
D7	Pin 2
R/W	GND
VDD/VCC	5V
VSS	GND

And for the potentiometer, we will connect the middle pin of the potentiometer to the VO pin of the 16X2 LCD display. The left pin of the potentiometer will be in common to the VCC/VSS pin of the LCD display. The right pin of the potentiometer will be in common to the VSS and R/W pin of the LCD display. See the following circuit diagram for clarification:

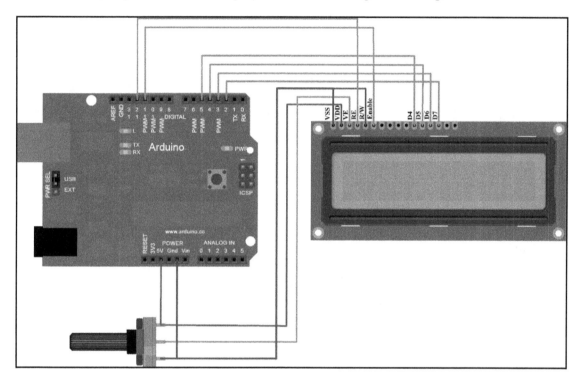

Now that we have connected the LCD display to the Arduino board, we will now use the Liquidcrystal library to display something on the LCD board.

Uses of LiquidCrystal Library

We use the LiquidCrystal library for controlling **Liquid Crystal Displays** (**LCDs**). The Liquidcrystal library works best with the Hitachi HD44780 chipset embedded on the LCD displays. This chipset is too common to the text-based displays (cannot display any complex graphics). We have connected the 16×2 LCD display to the Arduino that supports the LiquidCrystal library. To print something on the Display we will first need to import the liquidcrystal.h library to the code as follows:

```
#include <LiquidCrystal.h>
```

Now we will define the pins of the Arduino board that we have used to connect the LCD display:

```
LiquidCrystal lcd(12, 11, 5, 4, 3, 2);
```

Here `lcd` can be renamed to anything you want. But remember we will need to use this in the future code.

Inside the `setup()` function we will say what kind of display we have connected to the Arduino board as follows:

```
lcd.begin(16,2);
```

Our display is 16×2, so we have declared our display with the column numbers and row numbers of the display.

Now we will print *hello, world!* on the LCD display. To do this, all we need to do is write the following line:

```
lcd.print("hello, world!");
```

This will print *hello, world!* on the LCD display. But we need to do something more for setting the cursor of the text on the right place. Before calling the `print()` function we need to set our cursor in the right position. We want to start printing our text from the first column and first row. This is similar to two-dimensional arrays. So the first column and the first row's address is `(0,0)`. To set this, write the following line:

```
lcd.setCursor(0, 0);
```

See the full code to print *hello, world!* on the LCD board:

```
#include <LiquidCrystal.h>
LiquidCrystal lcd(12, 11, 5, 4, 3, 2);
void setup() {
lcd.begin(16, 2);
lcd.setCursor(0, 0);
lcd.print("hello, world!");
}
void loop() {
}
```

Let's upload the code to our Arduino and see the LCD display. The LCD display should look as follows:

Let's print something on both rows of the LCD display. We will print *Learning C* on the first row and *for Arduino* on the second row. To do this, upload the following code to the Arduino after connecting the LCD Display:

```
#include <LiquidCrystal.h>
LiquidCrystal lcd(12, 11, 5, 4, 3, 2);
void setup() {
lcd.begin(16, 2);
lcd.setCursor(0, 0); // For printing on the first row
lcd.print("Learning C");
lcd.setCursor(0, 1); //For printing on the second row
lcd.print("for Arduino");
}
void loop() {
}
```

The Stepper library

The `Stepper` library is used for controlling the stepper motors. In case you do not know what a stepper motor looks like, the following image shows a number of them:

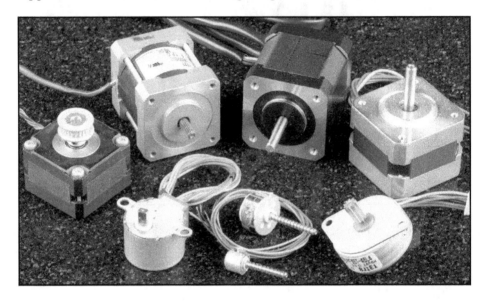

Stepper motors follow a very special mechanism to rotate. We can define how many steps it should turn on the code. To control a stepper motor using Arduino, we can use the `Stepper` library. There are two types of stepper motors depending on the phase number:

- Bipolar
- Unipolar

To run a Unipolar stepper motor, we need to use a driver. There are various types of stepper motor drivers. The drivers control the voltages and signals on the stepper motors. In this chapter, we will run our bipolar motor without using a driver and even library.

Let's connect a bipolar stepper motor to the Arduino, as shown in the following figure:

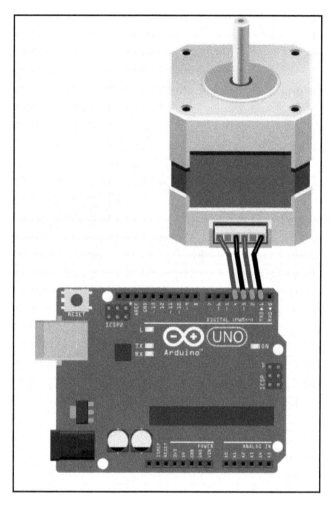

Now we need to define the pins we have just used. We used the digital pins 1, 2, 3, and 4. Define them on the top of our code:

```
const int a1 = 1;
const int a2 = 2;
const int b1 = 3;
const int b2 = 4;
```

Now we need to initialize the pins inside the `setup()` function:

```
pinMode(a1, OUTPUT);
pinMode(a2, OUTPUT);
pinMode(b1, OUTPUT);
pinMode(b2, OUTPUT);
```

Now we will send no signal to the pins (to hold the motor from rotating):

```
digitalWrite(a1, LOW);
digitalWrite(a2, LOW);
digitalWrite(b1, LOW);
digitalWrite(b2, LOW);
```

Since this is a bipolar stepper motor, each pin should get a signal once. Say a1 gets the HIGH signal and rest should get a LOW signal. By doing this, the stepper motor will turn one step. Now if we make b1 HIGH and the rest LOW, then the stepper motor will rotate another step. Therefore, to continue the spinning, we need to do this repeatedly. We can write four functions for four pins. And then call them from the `loop()` function. Thus, we will be able to run the stepper as long as we want. The first function may look as follows:

```
void step1 (){
digitalWrite(a1, HIGH);
digitalWrite(a2, LOW);
digitalWrite(b1, LOW);
digitalWrite(b2, LOW);
}
```

Can you guess what will be the `step2()` function?

Yes, the `step2()` function will look as follows:

```
void step2 (){
digitalWrite(a1, LOW);
digitalWrite(a2, LOW);
digitalWrite(b1, HIGH);
digitalWrite(b2, LOW);
}
```

The other two functions will have a2 and b2 high, respectively. We will call the functions from the `loop()` function with a few milliseconds delay.

The full code will look as follows:

```
const int a1 = 1;
const int a2 = 2;
const int b1 = 3;
```

```
const int b2 = 4;
void setup() {
pinMode(a1, OUTPUT);
pinMode(a2, OUTPUT);
pinMode(b1, OUTPUT);
pinMode(b2, OUTPUT);
digitalWrite(a1, LOW);
digitalWrite(a2, LOW);
digitalWrite(b1, LOW);
digitalWrite(b2, LOW);
}
void loop(){
step1();
delay(10);
step2();
delay(10);
step3();
delay(10);
step4();
delay(10);
}
void step1(){
digitalWrite(a1, HIGH);
digitalWrite(a2, LOW);
digitalWrite(b1, LOW);
digitalWrite(b2, LOW);
}
void step2(){
digitalWrite(a1, LOW);
digitalWrite(a2, LOW);
digitalWrite(b1, HIGH);
digitalWrite(b2, LOW);
}
void step3(){
digitalWrite(a1, LOW);
digitalWrite(a2, HIGH);
digitalWrite(b1, LOW);
digitalWrite(b2, LOW);
}
void step4(){
digitalWrite(a1, LOW);
digitalWrite(a2, LOW);
digitalWrite(b1, LOW);
digitalWrite(b2, HIGH);
}
```

Let's upload the code to the Arduino and see what happens to our stepper motor.

Installing a library

Installing library to the Arduino IDE is super easy. We can install a library manually or from the **Manage Library** option of the Arduino IDE:

1. To access the **Manage Library** option, you need to go to
    Sketch | **IncludeLibrary** | **ManageLibraries**. You will see the following screen:

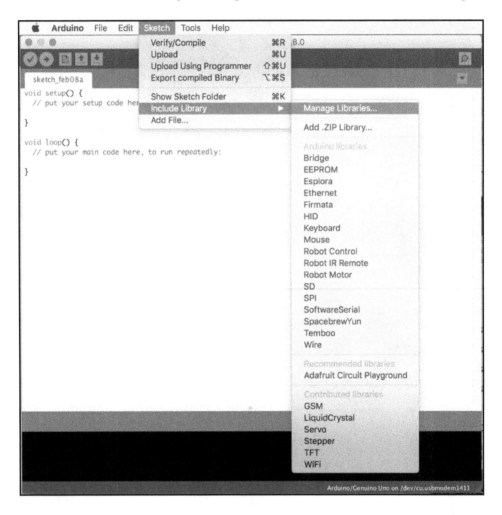

You can search libraries there and click **Install**. Say we want to install the *Audio by Arduino* library, search the library on the search box and select it. Now, click **Install**. See the following screenshot for clarification:

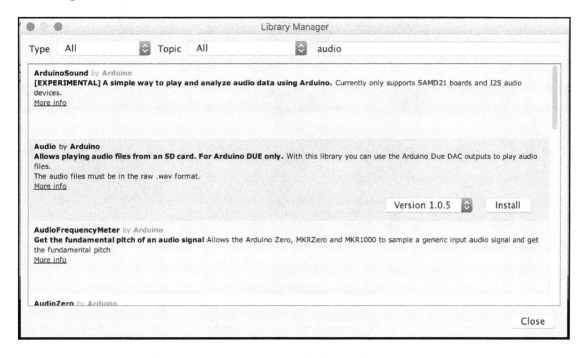

We can also manually install an Arduino library:

1. To do this, we firstly need to download the library from a reliable source. Say we want to install a library called `SSerial2Mobile`, to download the library go to `https://code.google.com/archive/p/sserial2mobile/downloads` and click `SSerial2Mobile-1.1.0.zip`. See the following screenshot for more clarification:

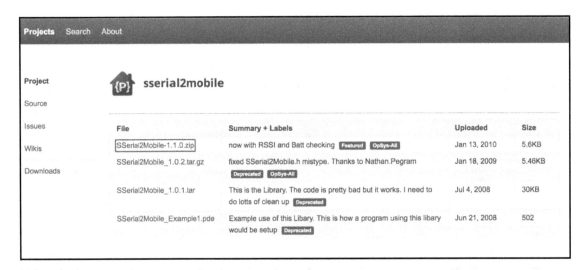

2. This will download a ZIP file named `SSerial2Mobile-1.1.0.zip`. You may extract it using any zip extractor software to see what files are inside the zip folder. You will see a folder named `SSerial2Mobile`. Inside the folder you will see a few files, as shown in the following screenshot:

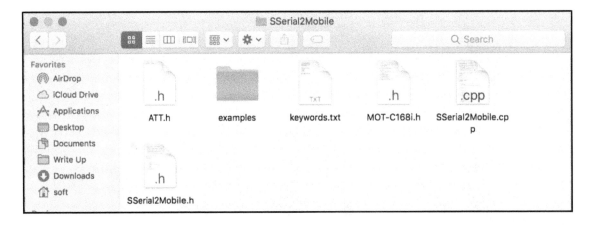

3. You can install the library as the zip folder. To do this, go to **Sketch | Include Library | Add .Zip Library**...

4. Then select the `SSerial2Mobile-1.1.0.zip` file:

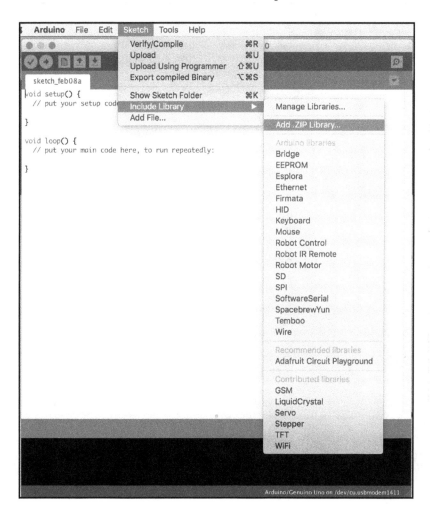

3. You will get the following message on the bottom part of the Arduino IDE:

4. If you see the preceding message, then the library is successfully installed.

5. Now you can get the library under the **Sketch | Include Library** menu.

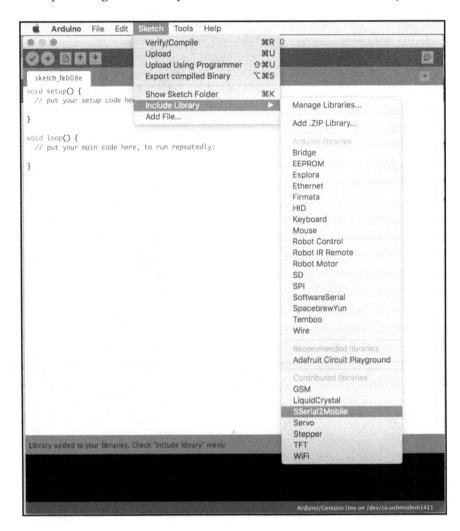

To get more secured and reliable libraries you can go to `https://www.arduino.cc/en/refe rence/libraries` and browse libraries you need depending on your hardware.

Removing a library

To remove an installed library, you need to navigate to **Finder** | **Documents** | **Arduino** | **Librararies** (on OSX).

Or **My Documents** | **Arduino** | **Libraries** (on Windows).

Or **Documents** | **Arduino** | **Libraries** (on Linux).

You will find the library you just installed. To remove it, simply delete it. The library will be removed.

Creating our own library

If we want to create our own library, we need to learn what kind of files and code make up a library. Every library has at least two files – a header file (its extension is .h) and a source file (its extension is `.c` or `.cpp`).

The header file contains all the functions of the library. It consists of a number of classes. All header files should include the Arduino.h file in the header file to get access to the standard types and constants of C for Arduino. So, the base structure of the header file is as follows:

```
#ifndef LibraryName_h
#define LibraryName_h
#include "Arduino.h"
// all the classes for the library goes here.......
#endif
```

We now need to save the header file as `LibraryName.h`.

Now, let's see the `.c` or `.cpp` file's structure. The `.cpp` file includes two headers. One is `Arduino.h` and another is our header file that we just made (`LibraryName.h`). The `.cpp` file then contains the functions of our main code just `LibraryName::` in front of every function name and *_pin* instead of pin. After saving the `.cpp` file all we need to do is install the library. Make a folder named after the library and put both the header and `.cpp` files inside it. You may make it `zip` and install the library as `zip`. Or you can just copy the folder (not the zip) to the following directory:

Finder | **Documents** | **Arduino** | **Librararies** (on OSX).

Or **MyDocuments** | **Arduino** | **Libraries** (on Windows).

Or **Documents** | **Arduino** | **Libraries** (on Linux).

After installing the library, you can include our library as follows:

```
#include <LibraryName.h>
```

And use the functions by calling them.

Summary

In this chapter, we have learned about Arduino libraries. We learned about a few famous libraries, and then used them with a few Arduino components. We learned how we can connect a Servo motor, stepper motor, and LCD display to our Arduino. I want you to play with LCD display and print all the things we used to print on the serial monitor. You can play with the Servo motors and precisely control things. I also hope that you build something combining the Arduino components we have learned to use. In the next chapter, we will build a number of things using the knowledge of all the previous chapters. If you ever feel the chapter is hard, do not leave, just stick to it and eventually this will make you able to be good in both Arduino and C programming language.

9
Lets Build Something Awesome

In this chapter, we will learn how to build a number of awesome projects including an LED cube, Smart Weather System, Home Security, and so on. This chapter will be the composition of the last eight chapters. What we have learned in the previous chapters will be implemented in this chapter by building the previously mentioned projects. Let's get started!

LED cube

In previous chapters, we were introduced to LEDs and learnt how we can use an LED with our Arduino. In this section, we will learn how we can use a number of LEDs. We will form a cube by using a number of LEDSs and programs with our Arduino to control all the LEDs from the microcontroller. Before going any further, let's construct the cube. We will build a 3x3x3 LED cube. This means that we will be controlling 3x3x3= 27 LEDs. The 27 LEDs will be connected in such a way that they construct a cube. Each side will have nine LEDs.

See the following image to understand the positions of the LEDs:

This is a three dimensional cube. From the image you can see that there are three layers (L1, L2, and L3). Each layer has nine LEDs. We will make three layers and then join them together. Let's make a layer first.

You need to make a 3×3 structure to hold the LEDs while connecting them and soldering. The structure can be made of wood/plastic/cardboard or any hard plane thing. You need to drill 3×3 holes on the plane surface as the size of the LEDs head. See the following image:

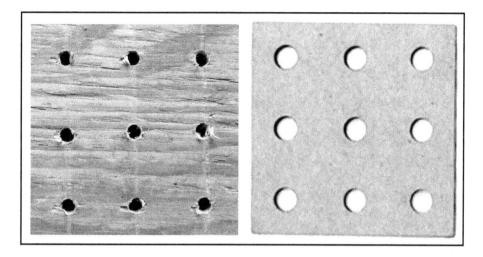

Now we will insert an LED to a hole (for my case, the top left hole) and bend the cathode 90 degrees to the right. Keep the anode upright, as shown in the following image:

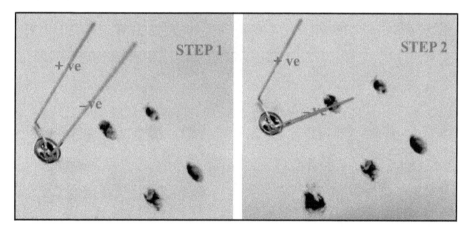

Now we will do the same thing for all nine LEDs:

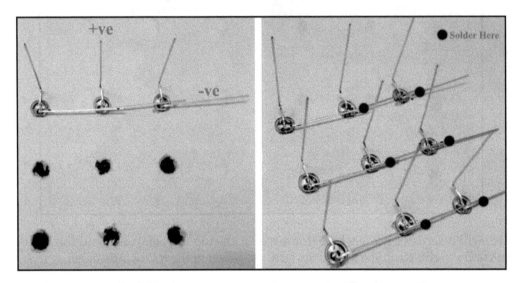

Now we will solder all the nine negative legs of the LEDs together with extra wires:

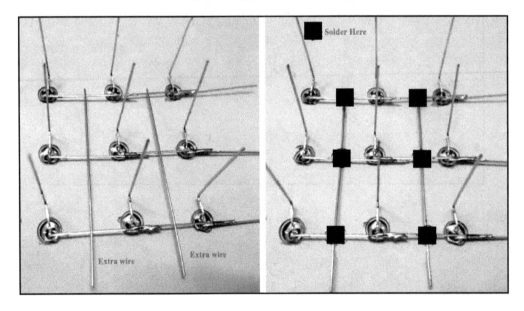

If we pull up the base now, we will see a structure similar to what is shown in the following image:

We will construct three bases and join them as follows:

Joining is easy. All you need to do is put a layer on top of the other layer and solder each joint of both the layers. Repeat the same procedure for all three layers.

Our LED cube is ready. Let's connect it to the Arduino now. Finally, we will have nine pins on the top layer and nine pins on the side of the cube. The pins on the side are common for each layer. So we will take out another two pins keeping one from each layer.

Now from each layer connect one pin to the Arduino as follows:

Arduino Pin A0 —————— Layer 1 Pin (The Bottom Layer)

Arduino Pin A1 —————— Layer 2 Pin (The Middle Layer)

Arduino Pin A2 —————— Layer 3 Pin (The Top Layer)

The nine pins on the top will be connected to the digital pins of Arduino. Before that, let's rename the pins as shown in the following figure:

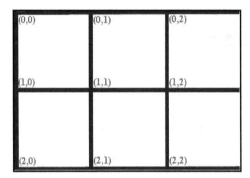

The preceding figure is the top view of our cube. To avoid complexities, we have renamed the pins. Now let's connect them with jumper wires to the Arduino in the following way:

Arduino Pin 2 —————— (0,2)

Arduino Pin 3 ——————(0,1)

Arduino Pin 4 ——————(0,0)

Arduino Pin 5 ——————(1,2)

Arduino Pin 6 ——————(1,1)

Arduino Pin 7 ——————(1,0)

Arduino Pin 8 ————————(2,2)

Arduino Pin 9 ————————(2,1)

Arduino Pin 10 ————————(2,0)

If you still find it hard connecting the wires, see the following circuit diagram:

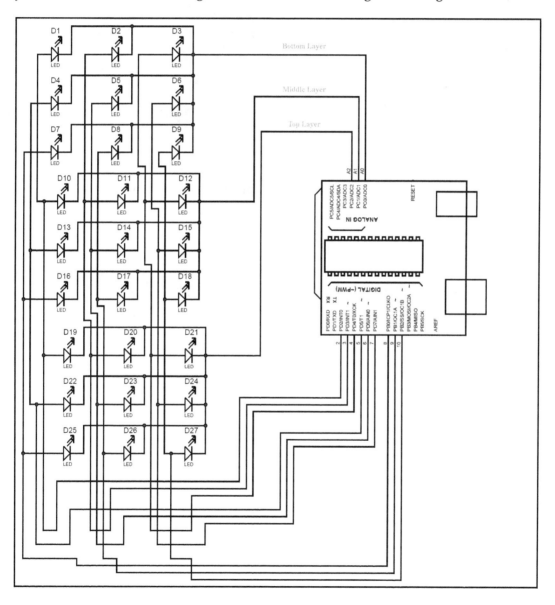

Since we have connected our LED cube, let's see how this cube will work.

If we want to turn on one single LED, say the (0,1) LED on the bottom layer, we need to power the bottom layer's common pin and the (0,1) pin on the top. If we want to power the middle LED of the middle layer, we need to power the (1,1) pin and the bottom layer's common pin. Let's write the code for the setup() function now. We need to set the pinMode first. We will set the common pins for each layer we connected on (A0, A1, and A2):

```
pinMode(A0, OUTPUT);
pinMode(A1, OUTPUT);
pinMode(A2, OUTPUT);
```

Now set all the three pins HIGH:

```
pinMode(A0, HIGH);
pinMode(A1, HIGH);
pinMode(A2, HIGH);
```

Make 10 reserved pins' output by running a loop for 10 times as follows:

```
for (int i = 0; i < 11; i++)
{
pinMode(i, OUTPUT);
}
```

In our loop() function we will repeat blinking our LEDs sequentially.

We will first turn on the first layer and turn it off after turning on each of the LEDs of the layer:

```
digitalWrite(A0, LOW); //Turned on the 1st layer's LEDs
for (int i = 2; i < 11; i++) //Turning on all the LEDs of the cube of the
1st layer
{
digitalWrite(i, HIGH); //Turned on the LEDs
delay(600); // a delay to see the blinking of LEDs
digitalWrite(i, LOW); //Turned off the LEDs
}
digitalWrite(A0, HIGH); // Turning off the 1st layer.
```

We will do this for all the layers. So what will be the code for the second layer?

Well it will look as follows:

```
digitalWrite(A1, LOW); //Turned on the 2nd layer's LEDs
for (int i = 2; i < 11; i++) //Turning on all the LEDs of the cube of the
2nd layer
{
digitalWrite(i, HIGH); //Turned on the LEDs
delay(600); // a delay to see the blinking of LEDs
digitalWrite(i, LOW); //Turned off the LEDs
}
digitalWrite(A1, HIGH); // Turning off the 2nd layer
```

Now it's your turn to build your own LED cube and run the following code and see the magic happen on your cube:

```
void setup()
{
    for (int i = 0; i < 11; i++)
      {
          pinMode(i, OUTPUT);
      }
    pinMode(A0, OUTPUT);
    pinMode(A1, OUTPUT);
    pinMode(A2, OUTPUT);
    digitalWrite(A0, HIGH); //pull up the A0 pin
    digitalWrite(A1, HIGH); // pull up the A1 pin
    digitalWrite(A2, HIGH); // pull up the A2 pin
}
void loop()
{
    digitalWrite(A0, LOW);
    for (int i = 2; i < 11; i++)
      {
          digitalWrite(i, HIGH);
        delay(600);
        digitalWrite(i, LOW);
      }
    digitalWrite(A0, HIGH);
    digitalWrite(A1, LOW);
    for (int i = 2; i < 11; i++)
      {
        digitalWrite(i, HIGH);
        delay(600);
        digitalWrite(i, LOW);
      }
    digitalWrite(A1, HIGH);
    digitalWrite(A2, LOW);
    for (int i = 2; i < 11; i++)
```

```
        {
          digitalWrite(i, HIGH);
          delay(600);
          digitalWrite(i, LOW);
        }
      digitalWrite(A2, HIGH);
  }
```

You can make your own animation and play with your LED cube. Let's move to another Arduino project.

Smart weather system

A weather system can determine a lot of variables and parameters related to the environment. In this section, we will stick to a few sensors to build a Smart Weather System that will measure air temperature, air pressure, and air humidity. You will need the following things:

- Humidity and Temperature Sensor
- Pressure Sensor
- A 16×2 LCD Display
- Arduino Board
- Jumper wires

The Humidity and Temperature sensor we will use here is a common sensor (DHT11 or DHT22). The following image shows a DHT11 sensor:

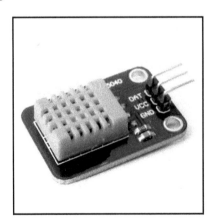

We will use a pressure sensor (BMP180). The following image shows a BMP180 pressure sensor:

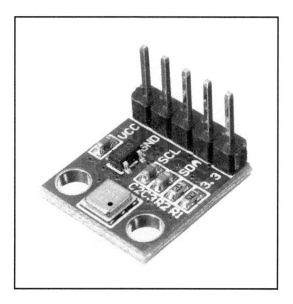

We already know how we can connect the LCD board. So let's skip this part for now. We will connect the other two sensors to the Arduino board.

The DHT11 has three pins, **GND**, **VCC**, and **DAT**.

Connect the **GND** pin to the Arduino GND pin, the **VCC** pin to the 5V pin, and the DAT pin to the digital pin 3 (or any digital pin you want). See the following figure for clarification:

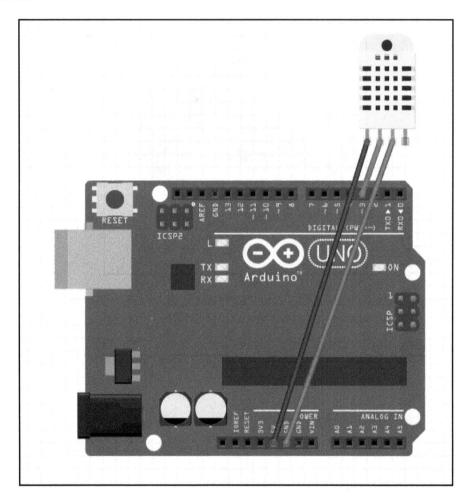

To get data from the DHT11 sensor, you will need to download a library (DHT.h). Go to this link https://github.com/SOFTowaha/DHT-sensor-library, and then download and install it to your Arduino IDE.

Let's connect the other sensor, BMP180. It has five pins, VCC, GND, SCL, SDA, and 3.3. We will not use the 3.3 pin. Connect the pins to the Arduino as follows:

- VCC to Arduino 5V
- GND to Arduino GND
- SCL to Arduino A5
- SDA to Arduino A4

See the following figure for clarification:

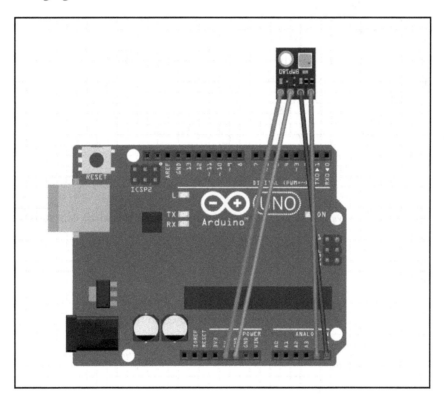

To get data from the BMP180 sensor, you need to download and install a library (`Adafruit_BMP085.h`). Go to this link `https://github.com/SOFTowaha/Adafruit-BMP085-Library`, and then download and install it to your Arduino IDE.

Now that you have connected the 16×2 LCD display, Pressure sensor, and the humidity and temperature sensor, let's move to write code for the system. We need to call the libraries we just installed to our Arduino IDE:

```
#include <DHT.h> // For humidity and temperature sensor
#include <LiquidCrystal.h> // for the LCD display
#include <Wire.h> //For communicating with I²C devices such as BMP180
#include <Adafruit_BMP085.h> // For the pressure sensor
```

We used the DHT and `LiquidCrystal` library. For the DHT11 sensor let's write the following line after declaring the library:

```
DHT dht(3, DHT11);
```

The first parameter is the pin (on which we have connected the DATA pin of the DHT11). The second parameter is the type of our DHT sensor.

For the LCD, let's write the following line:

```
LiquidCrystal lcd(8, 9, 4, 5, 6, 7);
```

Lastly declare a variable for the pressure sensor as follows:

```
Adafruit_BMP085 bmp;
```

In our `setup()` function we will write the following code to initialize our sensors and display:

```
dht.begin();
bmp.begin();
lcd.begin(16, 2);
```

Inside our `loop()` function, let's declare a few variables to hold the data coming from the sensors:

```
float t = dht.readTemperature();
float h = dht.readHumidity();
float p = bmp.readPressure();
```

Now we will print the values of the variables to the LCD display as follows:

```
lcd.clear();//This will reset the display
lcd.setCursor(0, 0); //Will set the cursor
lcd.print("T: ");
lcd.print(t, 1); //Print value of temperature
lcd.print(" C");
```

And for the humidity, we will write the following:

```
lcd.setCursor(9, 0); //Setting the cursor on a position
lcd.print(" H: ");
lcd.print(h, 0); //print humidity data
lcd.print(" % ");
```

For pressure, we need to divide our sensor data by 100 to convert it into Pascal unit. So declare a variable and assign the value to it as follows:

```
float hpa = p/100;
```

Now print the value to the LCD as follows:

```
lcd.setCursor(0, 1); //Setting cursor
lcd.print("P: ");
lcd.print(hpa, 0); //print the value of pressure
lcd.print(" hPa");
```

Now we will put a small delay inside the loop:

```
delay (2000);
```

So the full source code for this weather system will be as follows:

```
#include <DHT.h>
#include <LiquidCrystal.h>
#include <Wire.h>
#include <Adafruit_BMP085.h>
DHT dht(2, DHT11);
LiquidCrystal lcd(8, 9, 4, 5, 6, 7);
Adafruit_BMP085 bmp;
void setup() {
dht.begin();
bmp.begin();
lcd.begin(16, 2);
}
void loop() {
float t = dht.readTemperature();
float h = dht.readHumidity();
float p = bmp.readPressure();
float hpa;
hpa = p / 100;
lcd.clear();
lcd.setCursor(0, 0);
lcd.print("T: ");
lcd.print(t, 1);
lcd.print(" C");
lcd.setCursor(9, 0);
```

```
lcd.print(" H: ");
lcd.print(h, 0);
lcd.print(" % ");
lcd.setCursor(0, 1);
lcd.print("P: ");
lcd.print(hpa, 0);
lcd.print(" hPa");
delay (2000);
}
```

Now upload the code to the Arduino board and see the LCD display. Your Smart Weather System is ready!

See the following output in my case:

Let's make another project with Arduino for Home Security.

Home security

We will make a simple security device that will sense unusual motion in your home. Say, if anyone enters your room, the motion sensor will detect the human presence and make sound. We will also connect an LED too. You can later connect a GSM module to either call or send you an SMS if anyone enters your room. This time we will use the following components to build our motion detecting home security device:

- PIR (Passive InfraRed) motion sensor
- Buzzer or Speaker
- LED
- Resistors
- Jumper Wires
- Arduino

The following image shows a PIR sensor:

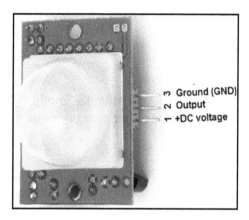

It has three pins, VCC or +DC voltage, GND, and Output or Data. The connection between the Arduino and the PIR is simple. We will connect the VCC to the 5V pin of the Arduino with the jumper wire, GND to the GND of the Arduino, and the Data pin will be connected to any of the digital pins. In my case it is digital pin 2. See the following figure for clarification. We will connect the speaker's anode to Arduino digital pin 3 and the LED's positive pin to Arduino's digital pin 4. See the following circuit for more clarification:

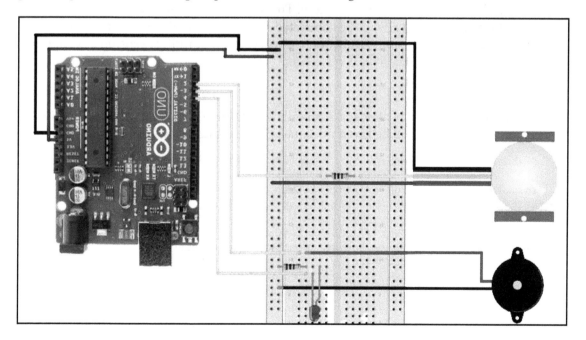

Since all of our components are connected, let's write code for our home security device.

We first need to initialize the pins on which we have connected the components:

```
int LPin = 4; // LED pin
int SPin = 3; // Speaker/Buzzer pin
int PPin = 2; // PIR Sensor Data pin
```

Before starting the setup() function, we will initialize another variable that will determine if motion is detected or not. So this can be either zero or one or LOW or HIGH:

```
int motionDetected = LOW;
```

Inside the setup() function we will set the pinMode as follows. We need to allow the PIR sensor some time to calibrate. So we will add a delay() function at the end of the setup() function:

```
void setup() {
pinMode(LPin, OUTPUT); // declare LED as output
pinMode(PPin, INPUT); // declare the PIR sensor as input
pinMode(SPin, OUTPUT); //declare speaker as output
delay(5000); //for calibration
}
```

Let's write code for the loop() function now. This will continue until we power off the device. So the device should always be connected to power if we plan to use it as a real security system. Inside the loop() function we will check if our PIR is sensing any motion by writing the following line:

```
motionDetected = digitalRead(PPin);
```

If it does, we will buzz the speaker and turn on the LED, or else the PIR will remain low and the LED and speaker will be given no signal. So the condition will be as follows:

```
if (motionDetected == HIGH) //If motion is detected
{
digitalWrite(LPin, HIGH); //Turn on the LED
analogWrite(SPin, 200); // Buzz the speaker with a tone
delay(100); // delay for LED blink
digitalWrite(LPin, LOW); // LED will turn off
analogWrite(SPin, 25); // Speaker tone will be changed
delay(100); //delay for a while
}
```

The code inside the condition will continue until the PIR does not detect any motion. If it does not detect any motion, the LED, speaker, and PIR will remain calm. For this, we need to write the following lines after the if condition:

```
digitalWrite(LPin, LOW);
digitalWrite(SPin, LOW);
```

So the full code will look as follows:

```
int LPin = 4;
int SPin = 3;
int PPin = 2;
int motionDetected = LOW;
void setup() {
pinMode(LPin, OUTPUT);
pinMode(PPin, INPUT);
pinMode(SPin, OUTPUT);
delay(5000);
}
void loop() {
motionDetected = digitalRead(PPin);
if (motionDetected == HIGH)
{
digitalWrite(LPin, HIGH);
analogWrite(SPin, 200);
delay(100);
digitalWrite(LPin, LOW);
analogWrite(SPin, 25);
delay(100);
}
digitalWrite(LPin, LOW);
digitalWrite(SPin, LOW);
}
```

Your homework is connecting a GSM module, an LCD display, a strong speaker, and 5-10 LEDs to this device. I know you can do this.

Summary

In this chapter, we have built three projects using Arduino. This is just a start and the projects are simple. But if you build them and add more components to your Arduino, who knows, you will build something really awesome. My suggestion is, just come up with an idea of what you can do with your Arduino, collect the components from a store, and then build it. For example, you can add a number of components to the Smart Weather Station project, such as soil humidity sensor, GSM module, Bluetooth module, Wi-Fi module, warning bells, and so on. Just think of what can be done to make a project more useful. In the last eight chapters, you were trained to do anything with your Arduino. From blinking an LED to building a super computer, all can be done with Arduino. All you need is to do what comes to your mind, and then see the output. If you find problems with code or hardware connection, ask the Arduino forums and search online. I hope no one would be able to make a better project than you with Arduino as you have learned C for Arduino with your best effort.

You might have faced a number of problems and errors in these last nine chapters. All possible solutions will be found in the next chapter, `Chapter 10`, *Few Error Handlings*.

10
Few Error Handlings

In this chapter, we will learn how we can handle all the possible errors we can get in the `Chapters 9`, Lets Build Something Awesome. We will also know a number of precautions for avoiding the errors. This chapter is designed by four sections, few common errors, cause of error, precautions and some advices. So, let⊚s get started.

Few common errors

Let's list a few common errors.

Arduino is connected but cannot be found by the computer

If you face this problem, then check the A to B cable is properly connected to both the Arduino and the computer. You can also check if the USB port is broken or if the Arduino's port is working.

If both the connections are good, then there might be the problem with the Arduino IDE installation. Just remove the Arduino IDE and reinstall the software again.

Cannot upload programs to the Arduino board

There are a number of things that are responsible for this kind of error. They include: the drivers for the board, the board and serial port selections in the Arduino IDE, access to the serial port, the physical connection to the board and more. Here are some specific suggestions for troubleshooting the problems.

Arduino software

Make sure you have the right item selected in the **Tools** | **Board** menu. If you have an Arduino Uno, you'll need to choose it. if you have an Arduino Mega, you need to select Arduino Mega from the list.

Then, check that the proper port is selected in the **Tools** | **Serial Port.** If you see the Serial Port is not selectable, then you can restart the Arduino IDE or start the Arduino IDE with administrative right. On the OSX, the serial port should be something like `/dev/tty.usbmodem621` or `/dev/tty.usbserial-A02f8e`. On Linux, it should be `/dev/ttyACM0` or similar or `/dev/ttyUSB0` or similar. On Windows, it will be a COM port but you'll need to check in the Device Manager to see which one is assigned for your Arduino.

Update the drivers

Drivers provide a way for software on your computer talk to hardware you connect to your computer . In the case of Arduino, the drivers work by providing a virtual serial port known as COM port. The Arduino Uno and Mega 2560 use standard drivers provided by the operating system to communicate with the microcontroller on the board.

The easiest way to check if the drivers for your board are installed correctly is by opening the **Tools** | **Serial Port** menu in the Arduino IDE with the Arduino board connected to your computer. Additional menu items should appear relative to when you open the menu without the Arduino connected to your computer. Note that it shouldn't matter what name the Arduino board's serial port gets assigned as long as that's the one you pick from the menu.

On Windows 7 (particularly the 64-bit version), you might need to go into the Device Manager and update the drivers for Arduino. Just right-click on the device and point Windows at the appropriate `.inf` file again. The `.inf` file is in the drivers/directory of the Arduino software (not in the FTDI USB Drivers sub-directory for it).

On Linux, the Uno and Mega 2560 show up as devices in the form `/dev/ttyACM0`. These are not supported by the standard version of the `RXTX` library that the Arduino software uses for serial communication. The Arduino software download for Linux includes a version of the `RXTX` library, which is patched to also search for these `/dev/ttyACM*` devices. There's also an Ubuntu package (`rxtx 2.2pre2-3`) that includes support for these devices. If, however, you're using the `RXTX` package from your distribution, you may need to symlink from `/dev/ttyACM0` to `/dev/ttyUSB0`, for example, so that the serial port appears in the Arduino software.

Run:

```
sudo usermod -a -G tty yourUserName
sudo usermod -a -G dialout yourUserName
```

Log off and log on again for the changes to take effect.

Access to the serial port

On Windows, if the software is slow to start or crashes on launch, or the Tools menu is slow to open, you may need to disable the Bluetooth serial ports or other networked COM ports in the Device Manager. The Arduino software scans all the serial (COM) ports on your computer when it starts and when you open the Tools menu, and these networked ports can sometimes cause large delays or crashes.

Check that you're not running any programs that scan all serial ports, such as USB cellular Wifi dongle software, PDA sync applications, Bluetooth USB drivers, virtual daemon tools, and so on.

Make sure you don't have firewall software that blocks access to the serial port. You may need to quit Processing, PD, vvvv, etc. if you're using them to read data over the USB or serial connection to the Arduino board.

On Linux, you might need to try running the Arduino software as root, at least temporarily to see if fixes the upload.

Physical connection

First make sure your board is on (that the green LED is on) and connected to the computer.

The Arduino Uno and Mega 2560 may have trouble connecting to a Mac through a USB hub. If nothing appears in your **Tools** | **Serial Port** menu, try plugging the board directly into your computer and restarting the Arduino IDE.

Disconnect digital pins 0 and 1 while uploading, as they are shared with serial communication with the computer After uploading the code, you may reconnect the pins. You can also do the followings:

- Try uploading with nothing connected to the board (apart from the USB cable, of course).
- Make sure the board isn't touching anything metallic or conductive
- Try a different USB cable: sometimes they don't work

Auto-reset

If you have a board that doesn't support auto-reset, make sure that you reset the board a couple of seconds before uploading. You can also keep pressing the physical reset button on the Arduino board while uploading the code to the board.

Bootloader

Make sure there's a bootloader burned on your Arduino board. To check this, reset the board. The built-in L LED (which is connected to pin 13) should blink. If it doesn't, there may not be a bootloader on your board.

java.lang.StackOverflowError

The Arduino environment does some preliminary processing on your sketch by manipulating the code using regular expressions. This sometimes gets confused by certain strings of text. If you see an error like:

```
java.lang.StackOverflowError
at java.util.Vector.addElement(Unknown Source)
at java.util.Stack.push(Unknown Source)
at com.oroinc.text.regex.Perl5Matcher.
_pushState(Perl5Matcher.java)
```

or:

```
at com.oroinc.text.regex.Perl5Matcher.
    _match(Perl5Matcher.java)
at com.oroinc.text.regex.Perl5Matcher.
    _match(Perl5Matcher.java)
at com.oroinc.text.regex.Perl5Matcher.
    _match(Perl5Matcher.java)
at com.oroinc.text.regex.Perl5Matcher.
    _match(Perl5Matcher.java)
at com.oroinc.text.regex.Perl5Matcher.
    _match(Perl5Matcher.java)
at com.oroinc.text.regex.Perl5Matcher.
    _match(Perl5Matcher.java)
at com.oroinc.text.regex.Perl5Matcher.
    _match(Perl5Matcher.java)
```

This is what's happening. Look for unusual sequences involving double quotes ("), single quotes ('), backslashes (\), comments, and so on. For example, missing quotes can cause problems and so can the sequence '"' (use '"' instead).

Arduino software freeze when I try to upload a program

This might be caused by a conflict with the Logitech process LVPrcSrv.exe. Open the Task Manager and see if this program is running, and if so, kill it before attempting the upload.

Board doesn't turn on (the green power LED doesn't light up)

If you're using an older USB board, make sure that the jumper (little plastic piece near the USB plug) is on the correct pins. If you're powering the board with an external power supply, the jumper should be on the two pins closest to the power plug. If you're powering the board through the USB, the jumper should be on the two pins closest to the USB plug.

Get an error when launching arduino.exe on Windows

If you get an error when double-clicking the arduino.exe executable on Windows, for example:

Arduino has encountered a problem and needs to close.

you'll need to launch Arduino using the run.bat file. You need to be patient, the Arduino environment may take some time to open.

Could not find the main class

You may get the following error when launching Arduino:

```
Java Virtual Machine Launcher: Could not find the main class. Program will
exit
```

Make sure that you correctly extracted all the contents of the `Arduino.zip` file – in particular that the lib directory is directly inside of the Arduino directory and contains the file `pde.jar`. If the problem still occurs, you can reinstall the installer file of Arduino IDE other than downloading the portable file.

Cygwin conflicts on Windows

Arduino IDE conflicts with Cygwin. If you already have cygwin installed on your machine, you might get an error like this when you try to compile a sketch in Arduino:

```
6 [main] ? (3512) C:\Dev\arduino-0006\tools\avr\bin\avr-gcc.exe: *** fatal
error - C:\Dev\arduino-0006\tools\avr\bin\avr-gcc.exe: *** system shared
memory version mismatch detected - 0x75BE0084/0x75BE009C
```

This problem is probably due to using incompatible versions of the Cygwin dynamic link library file.

Search for the `cygwin1.dll` using the Windows Start->Find/Search facility and delete all but the most recent version. The most recent version should reside in `x:\cygwin\bin`, where *x* is the drive on which you have installed the Cygwin distribution. Rebooting is also suggested if you are unable to find another Cygwin DLL.

If so, first make sure that you don't have Cygwin running when you use Arduino. If that doesn't help, you can try deleting `cygwin1.dll` from the Arduino directory and replacing it with the `cygwin1.dll` from your existing Cygwin installation (it is probably in `c:\cygwin\bin`).

Tools | Serial Port menu is not visible

If you're using a USB Arduino board, make sure you have installed all the required drivers.

Make sure that the board is plugged in: the serial port menu refreshes whenever you open the Tools menu, so if you just unplugged the board, it won't be in the menu.

Check that you're not running any programs that scan all serial ports, such as PDA sync applications, Bluetooth USB drivers (for example, BlueSoleil), virtual daemon tools, and so on.

On Windows, the COM port assigned to the board may be too high. As described in Zeveland:

On the Mac, if you have an old version of the FTDI drivers, you may need to remove them and reinstall the latest version:

gnu.io.PortInUseException on Mac

```
Error inside Serial.<init>()
gnu.io.PortInUseException: Unknown
Application
at gnu.io.CommPortIdentifier.open
  (CommPortIdentifier.java:354)
at processing.app.Serial.<init>
  (Serial.java:127)
at processing.app.Serial.<init>(Serial.java:72)
```

This probably means that the port is actually in use by another application. Please make sure that you're not running other programs that access serial or USB ports, such as PDA sync applications, Bluetooth device managers, certain firewalls, etc. Also, note that some programs (for example, Max/MSP) keep the serial port open even when not using it-you may to need to close any patches that use the serial port or quit the application entirely.

If you get this error with Arduino 0004 or earlier, or with Processing, you'll need to run the `macosx_setup.command` and then restart your computer. Arduino 0004 includes a modified version of this script that all users need to run (even those who ran the one that came with Arduino 0003). You may also need to delete the contents of the `/var/spool/uucp` directory.

Sketch appear to upload successfully but not do anything

This means you have selected the wrong item from the **Tools | Microcontroller** menu. Make sure that the selected microcontroller corresponds to the one on your board (either ATmega8 or ATmega168)-the name will be written on the largest chip on the board.

Check for a noisy power supply. It's possible that this could cause the chip to lose its sketch.

Alternatively, the sketch may be too big for the board. When uploading your sketch, Arduino 0004 checks if it's too big for the ATmega8, but it bases its calculation on a 1 Kb bootloader. You may have an older bootloader that takes up 2 Kb of the 8 Kb of program space (flash) on the ATmega8 instead of the 1 Kb used by the current bootloader. If yours is bigger, only part of the sketch will be uploaded, but the software won't know and your board will continually reset, pause, reset.

If you have access to an AVR-ISP or parallel port programmer, you can burn the latest version of the bootloader to your board with the **Tools | Burn Bootloader** menu item. Otherwise, you can tell the Arduino environment the amount of space available for sketches by editing the `upload.maximum_size` variable in your preferences file. Change 7168 to 6144, and the environment should correctly warn you when your sketch is too big.

Not getting a PWM (an analog output) when I call `analogWrite()` on pins other than 3, 5, 6, 9, 10, or 11

The microcontroller on the Arduino board (the ATmega168) only supports PWM/analogWrite() on certain pins. Calling `analogWrite()` on any other pins will give high (5 volts) for values greater than 128 and low (0 volts) for values less than 128. (Older Arduino boards with an ATmega8 only support PWM output on pins 9, 10, and 11.)

Undeclared functions or undeclared types error

The Arduino environment attempts to automatically generate prototypes for your functions, so that you can order them how you like in your sketch. This process, however, isn't perfect, and sometimes leads to obscure error messages.

If you declare a custom type in your code, and create a function that accepts or returns a value of that type, you'll get an error when you try to compile the sketch. This is because the automatically generated prototype for that function will appear above the type definition.

If you declare a function with a two-word return type (for example, `unsigned int`), the environment will not realize it's a function and will not create a prototype for it. That means you need to provide your own, or place the definition of the function above any calls to it.

Invalid device signature when trying to upload a sketch

This can mean one of two things. Either you have the wrong board selected from the **Tools | Board** menu or you're not using the right version of avr. Arduino uses a slightly modified version of avr to upload sketches to the Arduino board. The standard version queries for the board's device signature in a way that is not understood by the bootloader, resulting in this error. Make sure you're using the version of avr that comes with Arduino. (Don⊙t worry about it if your make a fresh install of the Arduino IDE and use a newer board)

'xxx' does not name a type error

This is the most common library-related error message and it means that the compiler could not find the library. This can be due to:

Library is not Installed properly

You must download and install the entire library. Do not omit or alter the names of any files inside the library folder. Make sure you install the library as shown in the previous chapters.

Wrong folder location

The IDE will not load files with certain characters in the name. When you unzip the file, rename the folder so that it does not contain any *illegal* characters.

Library dependencies

Some Libraries are dependent on other libraries. For example, most of the Adafruit Graphic Display libraries are dependent on the Adafruit GFX Library. You must have the GFX library installed to use the dependent libraries.

Wrong library name

The name specified in the #include of your sketch must match exactly (including capitalization!) the class name in the library. If it does not match exactly, the IDE will not be able to find it. The example sketches included with the library will have the correct spelling. Just cut and paste from there to avoid typos.

Wrong folder name

The IDE will not load files with certain characters in the name. Unfortunately, it doesn't like the dashes in the zip files' names generated by Github. When you unzip the file, rename the folder so that it does not contain any "illegal" characters. Simply replacing each dash ("-") with an underscore ("_") usually works.

Forgot to close the Arduino IDE

The IDE only searches for libraries at startup. You must shut down ALL instances of the IDE and restart it before it will recognize a newly installed library.

 For Future, Be careful

Check your hardware connections

Always check if any of the connection are loose or not open. Say, for example, you want to connect an LCD display with the Arduino, but you got confused about the connection of the wires. Check several times whether you are making the correct connections. Also check for short circuits.

Check the coding syntax error

The most common problem for a programmer is missing semicolons at the end of a line. The second most common error is missing the curly bracket. Also, try to avoid typos or your code will never run properly. Follow the log for the Arduino IDE to debug the error. And, since Arduino code is case sensitive, you must not mix up capital and lower case letters while working with the coding syntax.

Use serial monitor

It is a good practice to use the serial monitor for debugging the Arduino code. You can watch what is happening on the code if you add Serial.print calls to your code. Serial Monitor helps to minimize coding errors.

Stay connected with the Arduino forum

If you face problems with any unknown error (that is, other than the errors and problems stated previously), you can always ask questions and get help from the Arduino community. The Arduino forum's web address is `https://forum.arduino.cc/`. You need to sign up there before starting to post on the forum.

Summary

In this chapter, we have learned how we can solve some problems that can occur when we configure Arduino for the computer, and other problems. There might be other problems and errors that occur in your installation. You can always contact me via email or can open a thread on the Arduino forum to find a solution.

This book is just a start with respect to microcontroller programming. You are now on your own to explore the world of C programming and microcontroller programming. I hope this book will create your base knowledge of Arduino strong.

Index

www.ingramcontent.com/pod-product-compliance
Lightning Source LLC
Chambersburg PA
CBHW062048050326
40690CB00016B/3020